Animal Rights & Welfare

Editor: Danielle Lobban

Volume 445

First published by Independence Educational Publishers

The Studio, High Green

Great Shelford

Cambridge CB22 5EG

England

© Independence 2024

Copyright

This book is sold subject to the condition that it shall not,
by way of trade or otherwise, be lent, resold, hired out or otherwise
circulated in any form of binding or cover other than that in which it
is published without the publisher's prior consent.

Photocopy licence

The material in this book is protected by copyright. However, the
purchaser is free to make multiple copies of particular articles for instructional
purposes for immediate use within the purchasing institution.
Making copies of the entire book is not permitted.

ISBN-13: 978 1 86168 905 4

Printed in Great Britain

Zenith Print Group

Acknowledgements

The publisher is grateful for permission to reproduce the material in this book. While every care has been taken to trace and acknowledge copyright, the publisher tenders its apology for any accidental infringement or where copyright has proved untraceable. The publisher would be pleased to come to a suitable arrangement in any such case with the rightful owner.

The material reproduced in **issues** books is provided as an educational resource only. The views, opinions and information contained within reprinted material in **issues** books do not necessarily represent those of Independence Educational Publishers and its employees.

Images

Cover image courtesy of iStock. All other images courtesy of Freepik, Pexels, Pixabay, and Unsplash.

Additional acknowledgements

With thanks to the Independence team: Tracy Biram, Janey Hills, Klaudia Sommer and Jackie Staines.

Danielle Lobban

Cambridge, May 2024

Contents

Chapter 1: Welfare, Rights and Laws

Is animal welfare the same as animal rights?	1
John Humphrys – animal welfare: are we too sentimental or too cruel?	4
How the world might look if animals had legal rights	6
Encouraging animal sentience laws around the world	8
The big idea: should animals have the same rights as humans?	10
Advancing animal rights	12
EU may scrap animal welfare plan over fears it will drive up food costs	14
Which UK laws 'protect' animals?	15

Chapter 2: Animal Testing

What is animal testing?	17
What is ethical animal research? A scientist and veterinarian explain	18
Animal research statistics for Great Britain, 2022	20
Where do Britons stand on animal testing?	23
Alternatives to animal testing: science, ethics, and the law	25
UK government confirms no legal requirement for animal testing in medical research	27

Chapter 3: Animal Matters

Zoos repeatedly failing animals	29
The animals that like visitors at the zoo – and those that want you to stay away	31
The horrors behind wearing fur, skin, and feathers	32
Why would anyone shoot an elephant for fun?	33
There's no such thing as an 'overbred' dog – here's why	34
Puppy smuggling crackdown and live exports ban dropped in major government U-turn	38
Dogs being killed, poisoned, beaten, and mutilated on massive scale, says RSPCA	40
Should we keep animals as pets?	41

Further Reading/Useful Websites	42
Glossary	43
Index	44

Introduction

Animal Rights & Welfare is Volume 445 in the **issues** series. The aim of the series is to offer current, diverse information about important issues in our world, from a UK perspective.

About *Animal Rights & Welfare*

While the UK can be described as a nation of animal lovers, this sadly isn't the case in other parts of the world. This book looks at the current issues around animal welfare in the UK and abroad, including recent legislation recognising animal sentience. It also explores the ongoing concerns of cruelty and ethics surrounding animal testing.

Our sources

Titles in the **issues** series are designed to function as educational resource books, providing a balanced overview of a specific subject.

The information in our books is comprised of facts, articles and opinions from many different sources, including:

- Newspaper reports and opinion pieces
- Website factsheets
- Magazine and journal articles
- Statistics and surveys
- Government reports
- Literature from special interest groups.

A note on critical evaluation

Because the information reprinted here is from a number of different sources, readers should bear in mind the origin of the text and whether the source is likely to have a particular bias when presenting information (or when conducting their research). It is hoped that, as you read about the many aspects of the issues explored in this book, you will critically evaluate the information presented.

It is important that you decide whether you are being presented with facts or opinions. Does the writer give a biased or unbiased report? If an opinion is being expressed, do you agree with the writer? Is there potential bias to the 'facts' or statistics behind an article?

Activities

Throughout this book, you will find a selection of assignments and activities designed to help you engage with the articles you have been reading and to explore your own opinions. Some tasks will take longer than others and there is a mixture of design, writing and research-based activities that you can complete alone or in a group.

Further research

At the end of each article we have listed its source and a website that you can visit if you would like to conduct your own research. Please remember to critically evaluate any sources that you consult and consider whether the information you are viewing is accurate and unbiased.

Issues Online

The **issues** series of books is complemented by our online resource, issuesonline.co.uk

On the Issues Online website you will find a wealth of information, covering over 70 topics, to support the PSHE and RSE curriculum.

Why Issues Online?

Researching a topic? Issues Online is the best place to start for...

Librarians

Issues Online is an essential tool for librarians: feel confident you are signposting safe, reliable, user-friendly online resources to students and teaching staff alike. We provide multi-user concurrent access, so no waiting around for another student to finish with a resource. Issues Online also provides FREE downloadable posters for your shelf/wall/table displays.

Teachers

Issues Online is an ideal resource for lesson planning, inspiring lively debate in class and setting lessons and homework tasks.

Our accessible, engaging content helps deepen students' knowledge, promotes critical thinking, and develops independent learning skills.

Issues Online saves precious preparation time. We wade through the wealth of material on the internet to filter the best quality, most relevant and up-to-date information you need to start exploring a topic.

Our carefully selected, balanced content presents an overview and insight into each topic from a variety of sources and viewpoints.

Students

Issues Online is designed to support your studies in a broad range of topics, particularly social issues relevant to young people today.

There are thousands of articles, statistics, and infographs instantly available to help you with research and assignments.

With 24/7 access using the powerful Algolia search system, you can find relevant information quickly, easily, and safely anytime from your laptop, tablet or smartphone, in class or at home.

Visit issuesonline.co.uk to find out more!

Chapter 1

Welfare, Rights & Laws

Is animal welfare the same as animal rights?

The difference between animal rights and animal welfare, explained.

Often used interchangeably, the terms 'animal welfare' and 'animal rights' are not the same thing. Animal welfare is often viewed as a step on the way to animal rights. That's because animal welfare involves improving the conditions of the animals used by people, whereas animal rights calls for an end to that use altogether.

Let's take a look at the differences between animal welfare and animal rights, and why they matter.

What is animal welfare?

Animal welfare can be viewed as either a means to an end, or an end itself. There are many people who believe that using animals – whether for food, entertainment, research, or otherwise – is perfectly acceptable, but that they should be treated well as they are used.

There are others still who call for the improvement of animals' treatment as a step towards a world with no human-caused animal suffering.

Both of these perspectives are advocating for animal welfare, but they simply have different end goals. Oftentimes, the two may find themselves working together in order to eliminate the worst animal suffering. At other times, the two parties can butt heads about what really constitutes animal welfare. For example, does keeping egg-laying hens in enriched cages constitute good welfare? We don't think so. That's why we're pushing for cage-free.

What are examples of animal welfare issues?

Anytime humans are keeping, raising, or using animals, there are likely to be welfare issues.

A welfare issue could be anything from a pet dog with an untreated ear infection, to a dairy cow with mastitis, or a piglet being castrated without pain management.

As the most heavily farmed land animal in the world, chickens suffer some of the most severe welfare violations. Chickens raised for meat endure overcrowding and often deadly health problems caused by selective breeding, stressful transportation, and inhumane slaughter methods.

Unfortunately, the story of welfare violations continues with egg-laying hens. In the UK, millions of birds are still spending their lives in cages, laying hundreds of eggs a year. The high production often breaks their bodies, leading to prolapsed cloacas and fractured keel bones.

Often overlooked, the lives of the fish many humans eat are filled with welfare issues that have been normalised as part of the food system. Wild-caught fish are often scooped out of the water with massive nets that crush those on the bottom. On fish farms, sea lice run rampant.

At the Humane League UK, we're working to eliminate the worst suffering from the lives of the animals raised for food, including both chickens and fish.

What are animal rights?

Animal rights advocates believe that every animal deserves the right to live a life free from human control. This belief is most often applied to livestock farming, research, and entertainment.

Many who support animal rights also follow a vegan lifestyle, which means refraining from using or consuming animal products.

What are examples of animal rights?

Those who believe in animal rights may call themselves abolitionists, as they believe that all human use of animals should be abolished.

While in its purest form, animal abolitionism would include the elimination of everything from keeping cattle for beef to keeping dogs as pets, not every person who believes in animal rights would go as far as eliminating companion animals.

What's the difference between animal rights and animal welfare?

An easy way to remember the difference between the two is to think: 'animal rights might ask for no animals to be kept in cages; animal welfare asks for bigger cages (possibly with an end goal of no cages at all!).'

Within the animal rights movement, there are those who are advocating for total abolition, and those who are advocating for improved welfare for farmed animals.

At the Humane League UK, we believe that the animals raised for food deserve better lives while we move towards a world free from animal abuse. That's why we advocate for layer hens to be cage-free and slower-growing breeds for chickens raised for meat.

Why advocate for animal welfare?

Many supporters of animal rights argue that animal welfare 'doesn't do enough' because it doesn't demand a complete end to the use of animals for human benefit. For example, rather than asking major companies to stop selling animal products altogether, an animal welfare approach asks those companies to do better for the animals in its supply chain.

Of course, while animals are raised for food, suffering is inevitable. However, much as we may wish, animal farming will not end overnight, so we're fighting to reduce the suffering of the animals in our food system as much as possible in the meantime.

This incremental approach is based on the understanding that gradual change in the right direction can make a huge difference. A world free from animal suffering starts with a world with less animal suffering.

Our work has already eliminated the worst suffering for millions of animals. We've pushed numerous companies to commit to cage-free, and gotten many others to pledge to reduce the suffering of broiler chickens.

What is the Animal Welfare Act?

In the UK, the welfare of vertebrate farmed animals is protected by the Animal Welfare Act 2006. This legislation makes it illegal to cause unnecessary suffering to any animal, and contains a duty of care; anyone responsible for an animal must take reasonable steps to make sure the animal's welfare needs are met.

Unfortunately, many of the worst animal welfare offences are considered perfectly legal, as they're standard practices on farms. Regardless of species, when they're slaughtered, animals endure unimaginable suffering.

What are the Five Freedoms of Animal Welfare?

The Five Freedoms of Animal Welfare, written by Irish medical scientist Francis Brambell in 1965 and codified by the UK's Farm Animal Welfare Council in 1979, represent the bare minimum of living standards that animals in captivity should have.

Unfortunately, despite claims to the contrary, animals on farms are rarely provided with access to all five freedoms listed here. A prime example of this are egg-laying hens.

Rather than completely banning cages for hens, the UK only banned traditional battery cages.

Enriched cages, which provide only marginally more space per bird, are still used to house millions of birds.

1. Freedom from thirst and hunger

A recent investigation of a Lidl supplier farm found several chickens who had died of hunger and thirst.

2. Freedom from discomfort by providing adequate shelter

Despite gestation crates being banned, mother pigs are still housed in farrowing crates for weeks while their piglets are weaned.

3. Freedom from disease, pain, or injury

In the case of farmed fish, the water quality is often so bad that they struggle to breathe.

4. Freedom from distress and fear

Imagine how scared you would be if you were taken away from your mother at only a few hours old. This is the reality for calves within the dairy industry. Conditions that foster distress and fear are rampant in animal agriculture.

5. Freedom to engage in natural behaviours

Across animal agriculture, sentient beings are being restricted from displaying their natural behaviours. For example, pigs are phenomenally intelligent creatures, but on pig farms, they are often housed in barren environments.

Simple actions to support animals

Taking a stand for animals, whether for their welfare or rights, doesn't have to be complicated. There are many easy ways to make your voice heard.

Petitions

Many petitions can be signed from the comfort of your own home, making them an excellent way to make your stance known and advocate for change.

Contacting companies

One tactic our campaigners use is approaching companies directly to advocate for then animals in their supply chain. Often, we need your help to attract and maintain their attention.

That's why we ask you to write to the companies we're targeting.

Contacting MPs

Our representatives need to know how we expect farmed animals to be treated. That's why it's essential that we contact our Members of Parliament to make our voices heard.

What's next?

Humans cause pain and suffering to animals, especially farmed animals. Better welfare is not only better for them – it's better for us. Most people who still use animal products want to know they were produced by animals who had the highest welfare possible. Improving welfare standards gives us more peace of mind so we can advocate for a brighter, animal- cruelty-free future.

The conversation around animal welfare is constantly evolving, and it features many different viewpoints, even from advocates with the same ultimate goals. Still, this ongoing dialogue and the actions it inspires continue to pull our society towards better conditions for animals.

27 August 2021

Design

Design a poster displaying the Five Freedoms of Animal Welfare.

Write

Write a letter to one of the organisations mentioned on the Humane League website, or to your MP to express your point of view on animal welfare. Make sure you use emotive language and use facts and statistics to support your argument.

Research

Create a questionnaire on views on the welfare of hens. Do people prefer buying free-range eggs, or are they happy buying eggs from caged hens? Find out why they may buy eggs from caged hens. Is cost a factor?

The above information is reprinted with kind permission from The Humane League.
© The Humane League 2024

www.thehumaneleague.org.uk

John Humphrys – animal welfare: are we too sentimental or too cruel?

Few things arouse such strong feelings, on both sides, as animal welfare. The papers and news bulletins have been full of the fate of Geronimo, the black alpaca condemned to death after twice testing positive for bovine tuberculosis. And there's been the controversy over Pen Farthing, the ex-marine who chartered a plane to rescue 170 dogs and cats from his animal shelter in Afghanistan. Animal welfare could prove a real headache for the government too. In autumn 2021 an animal sentience bill will be debated in the Commons. Hotly debated. Passions, as they say, are running high on both sides. Too high perhaps? Have we got our relationship with animals right? Are we too sentimental or too cruel?

It would be easy to dismiss the Geronimo story as just a typical 'silly season' thing the papers always get up to at this time of year [late summer]. News editors have little proper news to report so they grab at anything, especially if it allows them to fill their pages with pictures of cute, cuddly animals such as Geronimo certainly was. But this year the editors weren't short of news – anything but. And the issue concerning Geronimo was not frivolous, in the way that the skateboarding ducks of earlier silly seasons might have been. It was deadly serious. Geronimo had been twice-tested for bovine tuberculosis, a fast-spreading disease in animals and one that requires any animal infected with it to be put down. Geronimo's owner, Helen Macdonald, believed, however, that the tests had produced false positives and wanted a different sort of test applied. Government vets disagreed, there was a tussle, and eventually the government vets prevailed: Geronimo was killed on Tuesday.

But this was after a very public campaign to save him. So wide was the coverage that *Private Eye* ran a photo of an endangered polar bear clinging onto a last fragment of ice with a bubble from its mouth saying, 'Never mind me, how's Geronimo?' Protestors besieged the Gloucestershire farm on the morning he was taken, screaming at the government vets doing their job, and it took 20 police officers to shield them. Ms Macdonald declared that the government had always been 'planning to murder' Geronimo and a No. 10 spokesman felt the need to express sympathy, adding that such events were always 'highly distressing.'

The Pen Farthing case was on a different scale. Some years ago Mr Farthing, a former marine, set up an animal sanctuary in Afghanistan and when the Taliban took over he wanted to get his animals out to safety in Britain. So he chartered a private plane to do so. But he needed to get the paperwork sorted and find a way of accessing Kabul airport, surrounded as it was by so many thousands of Afghans also desperate to escape. He managed to get through by phone to a special adviser of the defence secretary, Ben Wallace, and there is a recording of him shouting and using threatening expletives at the adviser. In the end, he claims, the government didn't help him. He insists that he was interested in prioritising 'pets over people' – but the fact that he chose to charter a plane to save animals rather than desperate people has led to fierce criticism of him for getting his priorities wrong.

It was pointed out that if the Taliban were out for revenge and score-settling, innocent animals weren't likely to be their target. And Major James Bolter, a reservist in the Royal Logistics Corps, said: 'What do I tell those people left behind when they ask me why the UK put more effort into rescuing abandoned animals than in them? I have no answers. I am torn between anger and despair.' Others, however, have praised Mr Farthing's resourcefulness and his commitment to his animals.

issues: Animal Rights & Welfare   Chapter 1: Welfare, Rights and Laws

Human beings have long had a conflicted relationship to the animals with whom they share the Earth. It is reflected in the different attitudes of different religions. The Jain religion, for example, is so intent on making sure that humans don't harm animals that their practices go far beyond a strict vegetarianism. Many Jains wear face masks to prevent them from harming the smallest creatures in the air. By contrast, the monotheistic Abrahamic religions of Judaism, Christianity and Islam take an uncompromisingly robust view of who's boss. In the Book of Genesis it is written: 'And God said, Let us make man in our image, after our likeness: and let them have dominion over the fish of the sea, and over the fowl of the air, and over the cattle, and over all the earth, and over every creeping thing that creepeth upon the earth.'

Most of us have taken this very obliging Biblical injunction literally and exploited it to the full. In hunting animals for food it could be said that we do only what other animals themselves do. There's a food chain and we're pretty much at the top of it unless we're unlucky enough to stray in the path of a hungry lion or a lurking alligator. Nature is red in tooth and claw. But, using the manipulative intelligence that humans almost exclusively enjoy, we have taken these 'natural' processes to extremes. In Britain alone we raise and slaughter over a billion farmed animals a year for food, and consume over four billion marine animals. And it's not just to satisfy our stomachs that we exercise 'dominion' over animals. We conduct between three and four million experiments on animals. We keep ten million dogs and ten million cats as pets, we breed horses and greyhounds to race, and we imprison animals in zoos so that we can gawp at them. And so on.

Of course we haven't done this entirely without taking animal welfare into account. There is plenty of legislation on the statute books setting out the do's and don'ts of how we should interact with animals. And now there is a new bill before Parliament: the Animal Welfare (Sentience) Bill. What it aims to do is protect the rights of animals who are sentient – that's to say, vertebrates that have awareness, feelings, emotion and that can experience both pleasure and pain.

On the face of it, it is no more than a piece of post-Brexit sweeping up. When we were still in the European Union the issue was covered by an article buried in the Treaty of Lisbon. This bill, it's said, merely fills in the gap left by our withdrawal from the EU. Also, it's claimed, the new law will be extremely modest. All it does is set up an Animal Sentience Committee whose job it will be to monitor all government activity and offer non-binding advice if it thinks some proposed government action could be harmful to sentient creatures.

But opponents detect something much more far-reaching. They think it will provide a focus for extreme animal rights activism. Because the committee will be established by law, not just by the whim of a minister who otherwise could simply abolish it if it became too uppity, it will be a body which activists will incessantly lobby to promote whatever added protection they think animals need. And because 'sentience' is such a catch-all notion, they add, the committee will come under huge pressure to adjudicate in favour of 'feeling' animals. They foresee a renewed campaign against country sports. They fear the committee will stick its nose into proposed infrastructure projects, making them even harder to get off the ground, and they can see the committee throwing in its pennyworth against proposed trade deals if they think the country we're trying to do the deal with has lower animal welfare standards than we have. And, such is the way the world works, they conclude, the committee is bound to try to become too big for its existing boots. They point out (with some justification) that no such committee ever works towards winding itself up, but only towards becoming even more important. We'll end up having to ban the Grand National and close the zoos and so on.

And none of that might be a bad thing, say supporters of the bill. There is still far too much harm done to sentient beings in this country. Think simply of the hundreds of millions of farmed chickens who suffer lameness and serious pain in their legs in the last weeks of their short life. To most of us this goes on unseen. And there is much else that goes unseen, say supporters of the bill, and that's exactly why we need the bill. We must expose the cruelty we are still inflicting on our fellow creatures.

So have we got our relationship with animals right? Our exercise of Biblical dominion would suggest not. For one thing we have wiped out whole species by thinking we could control nature to our own advantage. Indeed we may well be in the process of wiping ourselves out as we destroy our own habitat just as we have destroyed the habitat of so many other creatures. Our cruelty is on a global scale and much of the time we don't even know we're doing it.

On the other hand, we are doing only what other animals do – exploiting the world for our own advantage and not being too squeamish about whether we hurt the feelings of other sentient beings when we do. The heron doesn't look too bothered about the feelings of the fish when it swallows it, so for us to be too bothered when we tuck into a chicken dinner is just sentimental (as well as being hypocritical).

Those, then, are the two poles of the argument. Where should we stand between them?

What was your view on Geronimo? And Pen Farthing? And do you welcome the animal sentience bill or not?

3 September 2021

The above information is reprinted with kind permission from YouGov.
© 2024 YouGov PLC

www.yougov.co.uk

How the world might look if animals had legal rights

An article from The Conversation

By Steve Cooke, Associate Professor of Political Theory, University of Leicester

Let's picture what our societies might look like if animals were granted rights against being killed, made to suffer or exploited for human gain.

When activists argue for animal rights, they ask us to imagine a different world. First, we need to understand how our lives are shaped by animals' lack of rights.

The range of uses we put animals to is enormous – going far beyond food, labour, and clothing. We use gelatin to treat paper, from loo-roll to watercolour paper. Tallow finds its way into our banknotes, animal hair gives structure to suits and milk protein is found in condoms and any number of tablets. Beeswax and shellac (manufactured by crushing countless lac beetles) are used to make sweets shiny and treat wood.

We even use waste from animal carcasses as biofuel.

Many religious and national festivals involve consuming meat or wearing costumes made from animal parts. Animal products are everywhere. We kill billions of animals to make them every year.

A call for animal rights is a call to forbid most of these uses in law. It is also a call to reconfigure our relationships with animals. Imagining such possibilities can be difficult.

What's the point, we may wonder, of even considering the ethics of a future we can barely imagine?

Thinking about it

One of the roles of philosophers working on animal ethics, I think, is to help us imagine. The humanities and social sciences try to answer the question 'so how would that work?' That makes ethical possibilities, even unlikely ones, the subject of meaningful consideration.

The first thing to say is that although granting animals rights would dramatically change how we manufacture products, many of us may not even notice. Not only are vegan alternatives available for most animal products, but advances in technology make the use of animals possible without killing them or making them suffer.

It is already possible to grow meat, eggs, milk, and leather in a lab without harming animals.

In the future, scientific advances will probably make widescale production possible.

One change we might notice though, would be an improvement to our environment. Animal agriculture uses vast amounts of land, water, and energy, both to house and feed animals, and pollutes our air, rivers, and oceans.

One worry we might have is about the loss of jobs and income generated by animal agriculture. The sector is worth billions of pounds.

Animal rights theorists might respond in a number of ways: one would be to say that we ought not to protect jobs and income generated from rights violations. Another response might be to point to the fact that intensive animal agriculture largely depends on terrible working conditions, often suffered by marginalised groups of people.

Animal testing

Similarly, most of us probably wouldn't notice a ban on the use of animals in most forms of scientific research. New

forms of animal-free modelling are now constantly being developed and many are well established. For example, advances in computer modelling allow scientists to predict how medicines will act in human patients without the need for testing on other animals.

Many people worry that we might not have achieved many of the medical advances we have without animal testing. This may well be true, but for animal rights advocates this isn't enough on its own to justify it.

A core purpose of a right is to protect the rights-bearer from being used as a means to benefit someone else. We can probably think of a great many deeply unethical practices that could benefit lots of people, but we rule them out because they would violate moral principles. In any case, if future advances are possible without harming non-human animals, then we ought to opt for alternative methods of research.

What about the uses we find for live animals, for example as workers, entertainers, and companions? Even though many people love their pets as if they were family, there are some people who ask vets to have their pets killed because they no longer want them.

Indeed, such cases are common enough that the veterinary profession has coined the term 'convenience euthanasia.' In these cases, vets do have the right to refuse to euthanise an animal. But there is ultimately no law to prevent vets from carrying out these instructions and many struggle with the ethics of doing so.

Animal rights

If companion animals had rights, then they would have to be treated differently. One possibility is that pets would become something much closer to a fostered family member.

We might even start to think of non-human animals as fellow citizens. As citizens, animals could be entitled to workers' rights, health and retirement benefits.

When the police dog Finn was stabbed by a robbery suspect in 2016 in Stevenage, England, the judge trying the case found that all he could charge the defendant with was property damage.

Although Finn's case did result in the law being changed to prevent harm to service animals being justified as self-defence, it didn't substantially change the status of non-human animals in law.

Full animal rights mean that dogs like Finn would be entitled what is known as legal personhood. In some parts of the world, such as in the case of the Magpie river in Canada, there are already mechanisms like this for natural entities.

Once, people probably couldn't imagine a future where slavery was made illegal, or laughed at giving every adult in society a vote. I suspect that one day we will look back on the way we have treated non-human animals with a similar sense of disbelief.

When we try to imagine a world with animal rights, it turns out not to be so difficult after all.

The concepts, technologies, and mechanisms needed are already in place; we just need to be brave enough to use them.

26 October 2023

Encouraging animal sentience laws around the world

Animal sentience is an important issue that, unfortunately, has not yet received full recognition and acceptance in legislation worldwide.

When we recognise animal sentience, we accept that animals can feel both positive and negative emotions. We understand that they are capable of experiencing positive emotions like joy and excitement. And we also know that they can feel fear, pain, and distress.

Recognising animal sentience isn't a purely theoretical or abstract concept. If we accept that animals can feel pain and distress, we must accept it is our responsibility to minimise experiences that harm animals like factory farming and the wildlife trade and entertainment industries.

Understanding animal sentience also changes our priorities regarding animal welfare legislation. Basic animal protections might ban physical mistreatment or violence, but sentient beings require more than just being free from physical pain.

Animal sentience legislation requires us to consider the mental and emotional well-being of the animals we share our world with. Let's look at the best examples so far, as well as some countries with a very long way to go.

Different animal sentience and animal welfare legislations around the world

Some countries have taken significant steps towards incorporating animal sentience into their animal welfare legislation. Here are some countries that have made great progress.

United Kingdom

The United Kingdom has come late to legislation around animal sentience, but the legislation it has produced is high quality. The United Kingdom passed Animal Welfare (Sentience) Act in April 2022.

Before this date, animals in the UK did have some protections under previous legislation.

The Protection of Animals Act 1911 and the Animal Welfare Act 2008 prevented specific ways of harming animals, including forbidding animal fighting and baiting.

They also placed a duty of care on owners and anyone responsible for the welfare of an animal. But none of these regulations truly recognised that animals were sentient and that their experiences were valid in their own right.

The Animal Welfare (Sentience) Act has gone a long way towards rectifying this. It recognises that all vertebrate animals (and an important selection of invertebrates) are sentient and that there is a moral obligation to protect their welfare.

Importantly, it also requires that animal sentience and welfare is considered when laws are being drawn up or modified. This is an important step forward, although it doesn't prevent policymakers from deciding in favour of damaging practices that harm animal welfare.

United States

The United States does not currently have any regulations on animal sentience at a federal level, although some limited legislation does recognise that animals are capable of experiencing pain and suffering.

Some states do have laws in place talking about both the physical and psychological suffering of animals and placing regulations and limits on how and when this is permitted. In total, 46 states consider at least some acts of cruelty to be felonies.

The legal position for animals in the US is that they are considered property rather than sentient beings in their own rights.

France

France was a genuine pioneer in the area of animal protection. Some animals were designated as sentient beings in the 1976 Law on the Protection of Nature.

The act only covers animals that have close ties with humans, specifically companion animals (pets), framed and domesticated animals, animals in laboratories and for the purposes of science, and wild animals kept in captivity.

Progress has continued since those first important steps. In 2015, the French Civil Code changed the categorisation of animals from 'moveable property' to 'living beings gifted with sentience'.

Although this is a welcome development, it continues to exclude wild animals, domesticated animals without an owner, and all invertebrates.

New Zealand

New Zealand also recognises animals as sentient. The New Zealand Animal Welfare Strategy took the first step in 2013 and this was then included in legislation with the Animal Welfare Amendment Bill in 2015.

In addition to recognising animal sentience, the act includes logical consequences of this recognition. For example, people are required to 'attend properly' to the welfare of their animals.

Canada

Animal sentience is not equally respected across all of Canada. There are some limited references to pain, suffering, and distress in the Criminal Code of Canada, but no overt references to animal sentience. The issue has been largely devolved to Canada's individual provinces and territories.

Some provinces, such as Quebec, are taking valuable steps forward. A 2016 Quebec law asserts that 'Animals are not things. They are sentient beings and have biological needs'.

This act isn't perfect, however. Although domestic companion animals must have their biological needs met, farmed animals must only be kept 'in accordance with generally recognised rules.'

There is some evidence of recognition of animal sentience in Canadian case law, even in situations where it appears to be absent from primary legislation. For example, some judges have referenced animal sentience in their sentencing decisions.

Progressing understanding of animal sentience and improving associated legislation can transform cruel methods of farming.

Peru

Peru has also chosen to include animal sentience as a principle in its animal welfare and protection legislation. In 2016, legislators passed the Animal Protection and Welfare Law 30407. This comprehensive law was remarkably clear about the status of animals as sentient beings and what that means for their welfare.

Article 14 states that 'all species of domestic and wild vertebrate animals kept in captivity are sentient beings.' This is a simple and unequivocal recognition of their status.

Article 1 asserts that 'the state establishes the necessary conditions to provide protection to domestic or wild vertebrate animal species and to recognise them as sentient animals, which deserve to enjoy good treatment by human beings and live in harmony with their environment.'

This is a significant step beyond most countries, who mainly seek to outlaw poor treatment.

Asserting a right to good treatment provides a good blueprint for other countries to follow.

Sweden

Sweden's Animal Welfare Act 2018 proclaimed that animals are sentient beings. It is an important piece of animal welfare legislation looking at how animals kept by humans and also wild animals used for scientific study should be treated.

One of the most exciting parts of this legislation is the assertion that animals have an intrinsic value of their own, regardless of the benefit they bring to human lives. This is a powerful and dramatic statement.

Unfortunately, it currently only applies to animals being kept by humans and for science.

While it remains a strong statement and guiding principle, the practical scope needs to be expanded.

Spain

Spain has also recently updated its animal welfare legislation, recognising animal sentience in the process. Law 17/2021 changed the status of animals from objects to sentient beings and family members.

The recognition of animals as potential family members is important in a range of different situations. An important example is that pets and companion animals can no longer be seized for non-payment of debts.

As sentient beings, their right to be free from distress is now being acknowledged and valued.

Stop countries stalling on animal sentience legislation

Despite the optimism in many areas of the world, animal sentience legislation is far from universal. Some countries have stalled in recognising animal sentience and many countries haven't started at all.

27 April 2023

The above information is reprinted with kind permission from World Animal Protection.
© 2024 World Animal Protection

www.worldanimalprotection.org

The big idea: should animals have the same rights as humans?

Debates about the human-like attributes of animals miss the point. Can we respect them regardless?

By Phillip Ball

The government has finally caught up with what most animal behavioural scientists have been saying for years by formally recognising animals as sentient beings in its Animal Welfare (Sentience) Bill. In November 2022 it was confirmed that the scope of the bill would be extended to include in the 'sentient' category all decapod crustaceans (such as crabs and lobsters) and cephalopods (including octopuses, squid, and cuttlefish). This ruling heeds a review led by Jonathan Birch of the London School of Economics, who points out: 'Octopuses and other cephalopods have been protected in science for years, but have not received any protection outside science until now.'

Although these rulings are welcome, their tardiness is sobering. People have been arguing fiercely, dogmatically and even violently about animal welfare for a very long time – yet framing the issue in terms of legally enforced rights comes with baggage about the socially constructed (and therefore exclusively human) nature of moral status and rights-based reasoning. The starting point should rather have been the nature of animal cognition: how we and other beings are situated in a broad panorama of minds. While there is still plenty to learn about that mindscape, Birch is right to imply that, given what science has already told us, it borders on the absurd that UK law took so long to formally acknowledge animal sentience.

There was, however, a long historical tradition of human prejudice and exceptionalism to overcome. Aristotle distinguished humans from other animals by asserting that only we have a 'rational soul', in addition to the 'sensitive soul' of animals. In the 17th century René Descartes notoriously asserted that animals are mindless mechanisms, so that we shouldn't mistake signs of apparent pain or distress as an indication that brute beasts truly feel anything at all. His supporters were accused of the most heartless acts of vivisection (although Descartes himself was said to be devoted to his dog, Monsieur Grat).

Charles Darwin's claim that there are 'no fundamental differences between man and the higher mammals in terms of mental faculties' didn't deter the radical behaviourist psychologists of the 1950–1970s, such as B.F. Skinner, from returning to something like the Cartesian view of animals as automata. (Skinner saw no ethical problem in training pigeons to be living guidance systems inside bombs.) Not until the modern age of neuroscience have we truly begun to recognise a continuity of neural hardware and cognitive ability between us and other animals.

Still the question lingers of whether there is some fundamental difference of mind that makes humans special. Certainly, the sophistication of our language, and perhaps in consequence of our culture, seems unique. But there's no reason to suppose that the capacity to experience pain, curiosity, empathy, and other felt aspects of existence belongs to humans alone.

> 'Sentience comes in every imaginable grade and intensity, from the simplest to the most sensitive, "hyper-reactive" human.'

Some biologists now argue that sentience may be a property of all living things, even bacteria and single cells. They assert that plants, despite lacking a nervous system, show signs of genuine cognition, even feeling. But if it is still disputed at what point in the living world sentience begins, the view expressed by philosopher Daniel Dennett is now common:

'Sentience comes in every imaginable grade and intensity, from the simplest and most "robotic," to the most exquisitely sensitive, "hyper-reactive" human.'

The concept of sentience liberates the debate from the more contentious matter of whether other animals are conscious: a question in which the obsolete Enlightenment view that 'human reason' is like a divine spark activated within us is still discernible. A ghost of Aristotelian exceptionalism remains in the suspicion that, while other animals may be sentient, only humans have that special form of it we call consciousness. The problem is that it's hard to assign clear, quantifiable meanings to these words – even in humans, where, for example, arguments rage over the cognitive status of people in a permanent vegetative state after brain trauma (that very term harking back to Aristotle's view of plants as possessing a mere 'vegetative soul'). Although we might not know or agree on what consciousness is, it looks increasingly peculiar to imagine it as a single and absolute cognitive attribute.

The question for animal welfare is how the evident differences in 'qualities of mind' between species colour our attitudes and obligations. One commonly cited criterion is whether other animals experience pain. American neuroscientist Joseph LeDoux argues that emotions such as pain are human-specific responses to physiological reactions: narratives we alone can create because of our linguistic capacity (for example, 'I'm hurting'). Others counter that, since all observable indicators of and responses to 'pain' in, say, dogs or chimps, look like those in us, it makes no sense to imagine some fundamental difference. At any rate, the humane position is surely to assume an equivalence unless we have clear reason not to.

And it's not just about physical pain. Experiments have shown, for example, that farmed pigs respond as if 'depressed' when kept in barren conditions devoid of mental stimulation, responding to signals (about food, say) as if they have acquired a pessimistic lack of interest in things that might benefit them. Again, we don't know what that situation feels like to a pig – but they do seem to have a response to their experience that displays a sensitivity to the richness (or not) of their surroundings.

One challenge is how to avoid framing this debate in anthropomorphic terms, to assess rights on the basis of how closely an animal seems to approach human-like cognition.

Cephalopods in particular have suffered from that tendency. The common ancestor we share with them probably lived about 600 million years ago – far more distant than that of all vertebrates, such as fish – and their nervous systems are very different: most of an octopus's neurons are in the arms, not the central brain. Some researchers think they might have a kind of dual or even multiple consciousness – a bizarre situation we struggle to imagine. Octopuses are 'probably the closest we will come to meeting an intelligent alien,' says philosopher Peter Godfrey-Smith. For octopuses do show signs of considerable intelligence, even if their motives can be hard to deduce. For this reason, in 2019 more than 100 experts in cephalopod cognition called for a ban on octopus farming in 'sterile, monotonous' environments.

In the end, the notion of 'rights' is hugely anthropocentric. Even the rights of, say, human embryos or people in untreatable comas (which might be argued to have less sentience than a chimp) are framed in terms of the potential for human experience. The Great Ape Project makes a compelling case for rights among our closest primate relatives: to not be killed (except in self-defence) and to be allowed freedom and dignity, habitat protection and freedom from intentionally inflicted physical and psychological pain. But while the often blunt instruments of law can be needed to prevent obvious abuses, the better question is not what animals 'deserve' or should be granted, but what kinds of mind they have, and what obligations we humans incur towards them as a result.

24 January 2022

Think!

Do you agree that humans have a 'rational soul' and animals have a 'sensitive soul'?

Do you agree with Charles Darwin's claim that there are 'no fundamental differences between man and the higher mammals in terms of mental faculties'?

Write

Write a single paragraph definition of 'sentience.'

Research

What is anthropomorphism? Can you think of any examples? Look for where the media has used anthropomorphism, such as in the news or in advertising.

The above information is reprinted with kind permission from *The Guardian*.
© 2024 Guardian News and Media Limited

www.theguardian.com

Advancing animal rights

With a particular focus on South Korea, Open Access Government explores the changing perceptions around animal welfare and some of the policies introduced to support this.

Animal rights is a controversial area for debate. For many of us, it is unimaginable for an animal to suffer pain at the hands of humans. However, in many parts of the world, whether for the purposes of tradition, consumption, economic gain, scientific research, or historical relevance, animals are still exploited for human gain.

In recent years, social media has helped to highlight the harsh reality and brutality that animals worldwide have been subjected to; activists and animal welfare organisations have used far-reaching platforms to encourage industry, governments, and the public to acknowledge that animals are not mere commodities void of emotion and that further policy action to prevent animal cruelty is vital to reduce their suffering.

The widespread increase in public awareness and publicly available information concerning animal welfare has encouraged many consumers to be mindful of the impact of their purchasing behaviour and for policymakers to introduce measures to mitigate animal cruelty in various settings.

Cosmetic testing, for example, has been an area of increasing public and political concern. In Europe and some other countries, it is now illegal to sell animal-tested cosmetics – though ingredients used in some products may still be tested on animals as per the Registration, Evaluation, Authorisation and Restriction of Chemicals (REACH) regulation, the world's most extensive chemical testing programme. Equally, while companies are prohibited from selling animal-tested cosmetics in Europe, they are still allowed to test products on animals outside of Europe and sell them in other parts of the world.[1]

Despite progress in finding alternative methods to animal testing, millions of animals are still used for biological research and to test the efficacy, toxicity, and safety of products, including pharmaceuticals, consumer goods, and industrial/agrochemicals. According to Humane Society International (HSI), it is estimated that more than 115 million animals worldwide are used in laboratory experiments every year.[t] HSI also notes that because only a small number of countries actually collect and publish data on animals used in testing and research, the exact number needs to be clarified. For example, up to 90% of the animals used in laboratories in the US are excluded from the official statistics.[2]

In South Korea, fundamental changes at policy level have been proposed to reduce animal suffering, including a ban on the slaughtering of dogs for meat – a longstanding custom in the country – and a ban on all bear farming from January 2026. National attitudes towards animal welfare in the country are shifting alongside a rise in the number of South Koreans owning companion animals. However, many, particularly younger generations, feel more robust policy measures are needed.

Changing public perceptions towards animal welfare

It is estimated that up to a million dogs are bred and confined on farms across South Korea to be killed for human consumption.[3] According to opinion polls, 85% of people in South Korea would not consume dog meat, and almost 60% of the population now supports banning it outright. While dog meat consumption is declining, a nationwide ban on the dog meat industry in South Korea is still under consideration.

Equally, according to a survey conducted by Realmeter on behalf of HSI/Korea, 81.6% of Koreans believe that legislative support is necessary to create and promote alternatives to animal testing.[4]

Ending unnecessary animal testing

Greater policy-level efforts are being made to advance progress in animal-free testing and in 2020, South Korea announced a draft Act that could position it as a world leader in non-animal testing technologies.[5] This new development was timely since statistics released in 2019 revealed an alarming increase in the number of animals used for experimentation in South Korea – a 187% increase in testing insecticides on animals and a 115% increase in the number of animals used to test industrial chemicals.[6]

Ms In-soon Nam, a National Assembly member, said: 'As a member of the health and welfare committee, I believe that this bill marks a much-needed initiative in our society to finally move away from relying on old models that use animals and collectively move forward to provide better research approaches based on human biology, which will advance public health as well as animal welfare.'[6]

The proposed Act on the Promotion of Development, Dissemination and Use of Alternatives to Animal Testing Methods (PAAM) was introduced in December 2020.

It would prioritise human-mimetic technologies to improve human health research and product safety testing. A second bill on the topic was proposed in December 2022. In 2023, campaigners submitted a petition with more than 66,000 signatures to members of the National Assembly, requesting the immediate enactment of the PAAM Act.

Although this marks a significant step in the right direction to reduce reliance on animals for experimentation, progress, according to Humane Society International, has been slow 'due to the lack of related laws and cooperative working structures among ministries.'[7]

However, what made this campaign concerning PAAM particularly poignant was the screening of HSI's award-winning film *Save Ralph*, which follows the story of a rabbit named Ralph used in a cosmetics-testing facility.

The Director of the Korea Center for Validation of Alternative Animal Methods at the Ministry of Food and Drug Safety said, 'We are aware of the importance of the bill that replaces animal testing and agree with its initiatives. As a government, we will do our best to provide support for its passage.'[7]

Last year, South Korea's Ministry of Food and Drug Safety amended its biologicals standard and test method guidelines to cease the need for Abnormal Toxicity Tests (ATT). The test, introduced in the 1950s to detect contaminants in pharmaceutical and biological products, has been deemed unnecessary and obsolete in many parts of the world following the emergence of modern pharmaceutical production and manufacturing facilities with clear and specific quality control measures.

The World Health Organization has also advocated the removal of the ATT since 2018 in the EU, US, and Canada. The test can still be waived for some products in Japan and India.

HSI/Korea's senior policy manager, Borami Seo, said, 'We welcome this much-awaited amendment that does away with an obsolete animal test. This test was required for regulatory purposes despite evidence showing its lack of scientific value. Korea has a demonstrated capacity to adopt and refine rapidly advancing technologies. With this important step, we hope Korea will move even faster, showing its commitment to developing new technologies and reforming regulatory guidelines with non-animal methods.'[8]

Further policy changes to improve animal welfare

In 2019, South Korea's Ministry of Food and Drug Safety announced it was drawing up a five-year plan (from 2020-2024) to improve animal welfare and introduce tougher regulations against animal cruelty. Part of the plan would mean research labs must monitor test animals and apply stronger regulations concerning their use for experiments.

South Korea's animal welfare legislation – the Animal Protection Act – was first brought in 1991. Its significant revision, which came into force in April 2023, outlined substantial efforts to reduce animal cruelty and clarify the definition of what actions constitute cruelty. This included tougher punishments for those who abuse or abandon their pets and screening owners of new and current animal shelters, as well as the shelters themselves, before giving them the authorisation to operate.

Despite this critical revision, animal rights activists and welfare groups have expressed concern over the robustness of the act and the need for administrative agencies, investigative agencies, and the courts to fully play their part. They also said that even those punished for abusing a pet could still have their pet back after a certain period.

In a statement released soon after the announcement of the Animal Protection Act, the 'Korea Animal Rights Advocates' group (KARA), outlined the worrying distinction between dogs seen as farm animals and bred for consumption and those viewed as companion animals:

'All the animal abuse punishment applies to pets and it does not apply to dogs that are bred for consumption,

'Many people are not aware that Korea categorises dogs into two, as pets and for consumption. Under the current law or even the revised law, we can't do anything about abusive breeding and slaughtering of dogs categorized for consumption. We can't punish the owners of dog farms that rear dogs for consumption even if they are feeding dogs food scraps.'[9]

With increased public awareness and those at policy level continuing to strengthen animal rights, it is hoped that changes will continue to be made to promote non-animal alternatives across industries and treat all animals with the respect they so deserve.

19 July 2023

References are on page 42.

The above information is reprinted with kind permission from Open Access Government.
© 2024 ADJACENT DIGITAL POLITICS LTD

www.openaccessgovernment.org

EU may scrap animal welfare plan over fears it will drive up food costs

Scaled-back plan may be proposed to reflect living costs hiked by Russia's invasion of Ukraine.

By James Crisp

The European Union may scrap plans for stricter animal welfare and environmental protections because the rules could drive up food costs.

Brussels had promised to stop practices such as the killing of day-old chicks, the sale and production of fur, and the use of cages for livestock.

According to the *Financial Times* (FT), the European Commission has now dropped the plans and a law designed to increase green food production across the bloc.

However, one EU official said a scaled-back animal welfare plan would instead be put forward to reflect the rise in food prices brought in after Russia's illegal invasion of Ukraine.

Joe Moran, Director of European Policy at the animal campaign group Four Paws, said: 'Some in the commission are worried about the cost.'

The EU executive has carried out an impact assessment into the cost of the new regulations.

The report said the rules would increase farmers' costs by an average of 15%, which 'may result in higher consumer prices' and more imports.

A proposed ban on killing day-old male chicks could add up to 52p to the price of a dozen eggs, while giving broiler chickens more space would add 10p, the draft seen by the FT said.

The commission said it was still committed to revising animal welfare legislation.

'Preparatory work currently underway covers the legislation for the welfare of animals kept and farmed for economic reasons,' it said.

The regulations are part of the EU's Green Deal, which was set out in 2019 before the war in Ukraine started and increased food inflation.

Since then the rules have come under pressure from conservative politicians across the bloc who see the environmental laws as too burdensome and expensive.

Dutch farmers protesting EU climate rules triumphed in regional elections in March and are gearing up to fight a national campaign later this year.

'Real danger'

Red tape for farmers has become a hot-button issue for the centre-Right ahead of next year's European Parliament elections.

Ursula von der Leyen, the president of the European Commission, recently signalled a willingness to relax strict EU protections for wolves, which she said were a 'real danger' to livestock.

She was accused of waging a personal vendetta against the wild animals after one wolf killed her pony in Germany.

The German centre-Right politician is expected to address her track record on climate change and the environment in her annual flagship speech on Wednesday [13 September 2023].

The animal welfare rules were drafted after a petition called End the Cage Age was signed by 1.4 million people in 2020, and another to stop fur farming got 1.5 million supporters.

'Democratic demand'

Mr Moran said: 'Animal welfare is the last straw in the wind that is blowing the Green Deal to bits. It has to remain.'

'If it does not happen the commission would be ignoring one of the biggest democratic demands in its history.'

Copa-Cogeca, Europe's farmer's group, said it could support some changes to the rules if they received financial aid and if imported meat faced the same rules.

The UK and EU agreed non-regression clauses on environmental and food standards as part of the Brexit trade deal.

But the rules will not reduce existing levels of protection, so the UK will not be able to impose tariffs on EU imports for breaching level-playing-field guarantees.

12 September 2023

The above information is reprinted with kind permission from *The Telegraph*.
© Telegraph Media Group Limited 2023

www.telegraph.co.uk

Which UK laws 'protect' animals?

By Claire Hamlett

Several legal cases have been brought against the British government recently for various failures to protect animals. Cruelty Free International lost a High Court challenge to the government for 'secretly' abandoning a ban on testing cosmetic product ingredients on animals. The Humane League has brought a High Court legal challenge against the government for breaching animal welfare regulations by allowing farmers to keep fast-growing breeds of 'frankenchickens.'

The government has claimed in both cases that it has done nothing wrong (the Department for Environment, Food and Rural Affairs (Defra) has argued that fast-growing chicken breeds are not inherently at risk of health problems) and touted, as usual, its 'high animal welfare standards.' But this, along with the abandonment of a range of new animal protection laws that were expected to be adopted in 2022, makes it hard to follow what the state of animal welfare legislation in the UK actually is. So here is a brief guide to help make sense of where various pieces of legislation currently stand. The primary piece of legislation relating to animal welfare is the Animal Welfare Act 2006.

Animal experimentation

Since 1998, it has been illegal to test completed cosmetics (for example, eyeshadow or lipstick) and their ingredients on animals or to market cosmetic products and ingredients that had been tested on animals.

But in 2021, the government said it would align with a new rule brought in by the European Chemicals Agency (ECHA), an EU agency which oversees chemical regulation, requiring companies to test some ingredients used in cosmetics on animals to make sure they are safe. This change in policy triggered the legal action by Cruelty Free International. The High Court rejected the case because the chemical regulations cover testing ingredients used in cosmetics on animals to examine environmental impact or worker safety when there are 'no non-animal alternatives.'

In medical research, potential completed medicines and their ingredients must be tested in animals before human trials can begin. There is a policy of 'replacement, reduction and refinement' to minimise the number of animals used in medical trials and avoid using them where possible, known as the '3Rs.'

Animals who are farmed

There are different regulations for each species of animal on British farms, but here are some key laws over which there can be confusion, thanks in part to industry marketing and political lauding of welfare standards that can mislead the public. In addition to the legal requirements of care provided by the Animal Welfare Act 2006, the welfare of animals who are farmed is covered by The Welfare of Farmed Animals (England) Regulations 2007 (as amended).

Cages

Cages are still legal in some contexts on UK farms. Barren battery cages for egg-laying hens were banned in the EU in 2012, but 'enriched' cages, which provide a little more space per bird and include things like perches to supposedly help them express more natural behaviours, are still permitted. Chickens raised for meat are kept in large sheds or are 'free-range,' meaning they may have outdoor access.

Cages known as farrowing crates are also used on pig farms. Pregnant sows are put into them shortly before birth and

can be kept in them for up to five weeks, until the piglets are weaned. They are barred metal cages that prevent the sows from turning around and only allow them to move a little forwards and backwards.

Transport

The Welfare of Animals (Transport) (England) Order 2006 is the main piece of legislation relevant here (each nation in the UK has its own version). Pigs can be transported for up to 24 hours without rest. For sheep and cows it's 28 hours with one hour of rest in the middle of the journey. For unweaned lambs, piglets, and calves it's 18 hours with an hour of rest in the middle. Temperatures must be controlled for journeys longer than 12 hours, but can reach as high as 35 degrees Celsius.

The Kept Animals Bill, which is currently passing through Parliament, has a clause that would ban the live export of animals (except poultry) for slaughter or fattening. Animals who, under this bill, could not be exported for slaughter or fattening (for example, pigs, cows, horses, sheep, and goats) could still be exported for breeding purposes. Though, we have shown that this new legislation would only protect around 4% of animals who are live exported.

Slaughter

Animals in the UK must be stunned before slaughter (apart from religious slaughter like halal or kosher), restrained for as short a time as possible, and not handled 'in a way that causes it pain or suffering.' Stunning can be done by penetrative captive bolt – used on cows, sheep and some pigs; an electrical current sent through the brain of sheep, calves and pigs; with gas – this is used to stun pigs and is also used on the majority of poultry to kill them outright. Footage recently captured by animal activist Joey Carbstrong of pigs being gassed with carbon dioxide shows the violent reality of what this is like for pigs.

Animal slaughter is regulated by The Welfare of Animals at the Time of Killing (England) Regulations 2015. Despite this law, our Scammed! campaign highlights how the system is built to fail animals and animals are regularly not stunned for the allotted amount of time and suffer greatly as a result.

Animals abroad

The Animals Abroad Bill was supposed to be introduced in 2022 and ban the import of foie gras, hunting trophies and fur. While the ban on hunting trophies (body parts of animals like elephants and giraffes hunted abroad) has been approved by Parliament and is now to be debated in the House of Lords, the bans on foie gras and fur have been shelved.

As always, for the animals.

1 June 2023

The above information is reprinted with kind permission from Animal Justice Project.
© 2024 Animal Justice Project

www.animaljusticeproject.com

Chapter 2: Animal Testing

What is animal testing?

An introduction to animal experiments

What are animal experiments?

An animal test is any scientific experiment or test in which a live animal is forced to undergo something that is likely to cause them pain, suffering, distress, or lasting harm.

Animal experiments are not the same as taking your companion animal to the vet. Animals used in laboratories are deliberately harmed, not for their own good, and are usually killed at the end of the experiment.

Animal experiments include:

- Injecting or force feeding animals with potentially harmful substances
- Surgically removing animals' organs or tissues to deliberately cause damage
- Forcing animals to inhale toxic gases
- Subjecting animals to frightening situations to create anxiety and depression.

Some experiments require the animal to die as part of the test. For example, regulatory tests for Botox, vaccines and some tests for chemical safety are essentially variations of the cruel Lethal Dose 50 test in which 50% of the animals die or are killed just before the point of death.

Which animals are used?

A surprisingly, large range of animal species are regularly used in experiments, including wild animals.

Only vertebrate animals (mammals, birds, fish and amphibians) and some invertebrates such as octopuses are defined as 'animals' by European legislation governing animal experiments. Shockingly, in the USA rats, mice, fish, amphibians and birds are not defined as animals under animal experiment regulations. That means no legal permission to experiment on them is needed and they are not included in any statistics.

Animals used in experiments are usually bred for this purpose by the laboratory or in breeding facilities. It's a cruel, multi-million dollar industry. We believe that all animals are equally important. A dog bred for research is still a dog who could otherwise live a happy life in a loving home.

Some monkeys are still trapped in the wild in Africa, Asia and South America to be used in experiments or imprisoned in breeding facilities. Their children are exported to laboratories around the world. The use of wild-caught monkeys in experiments is generally banned in Europe but is allowed elsewhere.

Horses and other animals such as cows, sheep and pigs are often supplied by dealers and may originate from racing stables or farms for use in animal experiments. The rules preventing the use of stray companion animals like dogs and cats vary from country to country.

Wild animals can be used in trapping and monitoring experiments in the wild, or they may be captured and brought into a laboratory setting for more invasive research, sometimes in the name of conservation.

What are laboratories like?

Laboratories are no place for any animal. They are typically sterile, indoor environments in which the animals are forced to live in cages, pens, or Perspex boxes – denied complete freedom of movement and control over their lives. Some animals in laboratories are confined on their own, without the companionship of others.

Our investigations show time and time again that, despite claims by the animal research community, life inside a laboratory is no life at all.

The science relating to animal experiments can be extremely complicated and views often differ. What appears on the Cruelty Free International website represents Cruelty Free International expert opinion, based on a thorough assessment of the evidence.

The above information is reprinted with kind permission from Cruelty Free International.
© 2024 Cruelty Free International

www.crueltyfreeinternational.org

What is ethical animal research? A scientist and veterinarian explain

An article from The Conversation.

By Lana Ruvolo Grasser Postdoctoral Research Fellow in Neuroscience, National Institutes of Health and Rachelle Stammen Clinical Veterinarian, Emory National Primate Research Center, Emory University

A proposed measure in Switzerland would have made that country the first to ban medical and scientific experimentation on animals. It failed to pass in February 2022, with only 21% of voters in favour. Yet globally, including in the United States, there is concern about whether animal research is ethical.

We are scientists who support ethical animal research that reduces suffering of humans and animals alike by helping researchers discover the causes of disease and how to treat it. One of us is a neuroscientist who studies behavioural treatments and medications for people with post-traumatic stress disorder – treatments made possible by research with dogs and rodents. The other is a veterinarian who cares for laboratory animals in research studies and trains researchers on how to interact with their subjects.

We both place high importance on ensuring that animal research is conducted ethically and humanely. But what counts as 'ethical' animal research in the first place?

The 4 R's of animal research

There is no single standard definition of ethical animal research. However, it broadly means the humane care of research animals – from their acquisition and housing to the study experience itself.

Federal research agencies follow guiding principles in evaluating the use and care of animals in research. One is that the research must increase knowledge and, either directly or indirectly, have the potential to benefit the health and welfare of humans and other animals.

Another is that only the minimum number of animals required to obtain valid results should be included. Researchers must use procedures that minimize pain and distress and maximize the animals' welfare. They are also asked to consider whether they could use non-animal alternatives instead, such as mathematical models or computer simulations.

These principles are summarised by the '3 R's' of animal research: reduction, refinement and replacement. The 3 R's encourage scientists to develop new techniques that allow them to replace animals with appropriate alternatives.

Since these guidelines were first disseminated in the early 1960s, new tools have helped to significantly decrease animal research. In fact, since 1985, the number of animals in research has been reduced by half.

A fourth 'R' was formalised in the late 1990s: rehabilitation, referring to care for animals after their role in research is complete.

These guidelines are designed to ensure that researchers and regulators consider the costs and benefits of using animals in research, focused on the good it could provide for many more animals and humans. These guidelines also ensure protection of a group – animals – that cannot consent to its own participation in research. There are a number of human groups that cannot consent to research, either, such as infants and young children, but for whom regulated research is still permitted, so that they can gain the potential benefits from discoveries.

Enforcing ethics

Specific guidelines for ethical animal research are typically established by national governments. Independent organizations also provide research standards.

In the US, the Animal Welfare Act protects all warmblooded animals except rats, mice and birds bred for research. Rats, mice and birds are protected – along with fish, reptiles and all other vertebrates – by the Public Health Service Policy.

Each institution that conducts animal research has an entity called the Institutional Animal Care and Use Committee, or IACUC. The IACUC is composed of veterinarians, scientists, nonscientists and members of the public. Before researchers are allowed to start their studies, the IACUC reviews their research protocols to ensure they follow national standards.

The IACUC also oversees studies after approval to continually enforce ethical research practices and animal care. It, along with the US Department of Agriculture, accreditation agencies and funding entities, may conduct unannounced inspections.

Laboratories that violate standards may be fined, forced to stop their studies, excluded from research funding, ordered to cease and desist, and have their licenses suspended or revoked. Allegations of misconduct are also investigated by the National Institutes of Health's Office of Laboratory Animal Welfare.

Above and beyond the basic national standards for humane treatment, research institutions across 47 countries, including the US, may seek voluntary accreditation by a nonprofit called the Association for Assessment and Accreditation of Laboratory Animal Care, or AAALAC International. AAALAC accreditation recognises the maintenance of high standards of animal care and use. It can also help recruit scientists to accredited institutes, promote scientific validity and demonstrate accountability.

Principles in practice

So what impact do these guidelines actually have on research and animals?

First, they have made sure that scientists create protocols that describe the purpose of their research and why animals are necessary to answer a meaningful question that could benefit health or medical care. While computer models and cell cultures can play an important role in some research, others studies, like those on Alzheimer's disease, need animal models to better capture the complexities of living organisms. The protocol must outline how animals will be housed and cared for, and who will care for and work with the animals, to ensure that they are trained to treat animals humanely.

During continual study oversight, inspectors look for whether animals are provided with housing specifically designed for their species' behavioural and social needs. For example, mice are given nesting materials to create a comfortable environment for living and raising pups. When animals don't have environmental stimulation, it can alter their brain function – harming not only the animal, but also the science.

Monitoring agencies also consider animals' distress. If something is known to be painful in humans, it is assumed to be painful in animals as well. Sedation, painkillers or anaesthesia must be provided when animals experience more than momentary or slight pain.

For some research that requires assessing organs and tissues, such as the study of heart disease, animals must be euthanised. Veterinary professionals perform or oversee the euthanasia process. Methods must be in compliance with guidelines from the American Veterinary Medical Association, which requires rapid and painless techniques in distress-free conditions.

Fortunately, following their time in research, some animals can be adopted into loving homes, and others may be retired to havens and sanctuaries equipped with veterinary care, nutrition and enrichment.

Continuing the conversation

Animal research benefits both humans and animals. Numerous medical advances exist because they were initially studied in animals – from treatments for cancer and t disease to new techniques for surgery, organ transplants and noninvasive imaging and diagnostics.

These advances also benefit zoo animals, wildlife and endangered species. Animal research has allowed for the eradication of certain diseases in cattle, for example, leading not only to reduced farm cattle deaths and human famine, but also to improved health for wild cattle.

Health care advances for pets – including cancer treatments, effective vaccines, nutritional prescription diets and flea and tick treatments – are also available thanks to animal research.

People who work with animals in research have attempted to increase public awareness of research standards and the positive effects animal research has had on daily life. However, some have faced harassment and violence from anti-animal research activists. Some of our own colleagues have received death threats.

Those who work in animal research share a deep appreciation for the creatures who make this work possible. For future strides in biomedical care to be possible, we believe that research using animals must be protected, and that animal health and safety must always remain the top priority.

23 November 2022

The above information is reprinted with kind permission from The Conversation.
© 2010-2024, The Conversation Trust (UK) Limited

www.theconversation.com

Animal research statistics for Great Britain, 2022

By Hannah Hobson

Latest figures show a decrease in animals used in research in 2022

- The number of procedures on animals in 2022 has decreased by 10% to 2.76 million.
- Lowest number of procedures since 2002.
- Mice, fish, rats, and birds account for over 97% of all procedures.
- Cats, dogs, and monkeys account for 0.2% of all procedures.

Today (Thursday, 13 July 2023) the government has released its annual statistics on the number of animals used in scientific, medical and veterinary research in 2022. The figures show that 2,761,204 procedures were carried out in Great Britain in 2022, 10% less than in 2021.

97% of the procedures were carried out in mice, fish, rats, and birds, whereas cats, dogs, and monkeys accounted for 0.2% of all procedures in 2022.

What is a procedure?

A 'procedure' is any applied to a protected animal for an experimental or other scientific purpose, or for an educational purpose, that may have the effect of causing an animal pain, suffering, distress, or lasting harm equivalent to, or higher than, that caused by the introduction of a needle in accordance with good veterinary practice.

How many animals are used?

The number of procedures carried out in a year does not equal the number of animals that have been used in procedures that year. This is because some animals may be used more

Animal research statistics
Great Britain, 2022

Research facilities in Great Britain record the number of scientific procedures carried out on animals each year. Procedures are categorised by severity, they can be as mild as an injection, or as severe as an organ transplant.

2,761,204 Total number of procedures on animals

1,512,210 55% Total number of procedures on animals

1,248,994 45% Number of procedures for the creation and breeding of genetically altered animals

Most commonly used animals

- **Mice** 1,971,262
- **Fish** 371,237
- **Rats** 185,749
- **Birds** 136,190

Animals with special protection

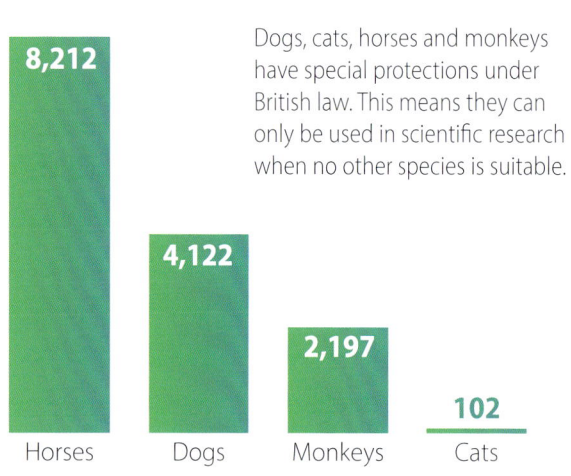

Horses: 8,212 | Dogs: 4,122 | Monkeys: 2,197 | Cats: 102

Dogs, cats, horses and monkeys have special protections under British law. This means they can only be used in scientific research when no other species is suitable.

Severity of experiments

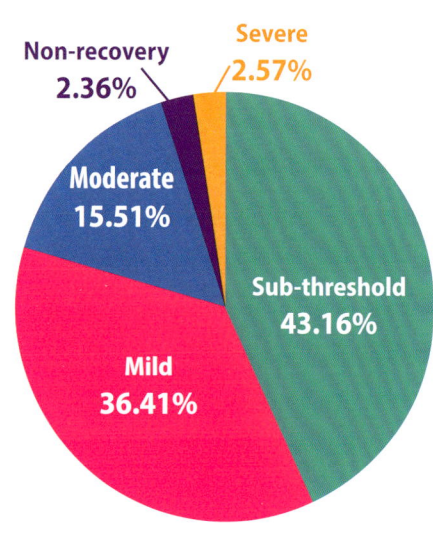

- Severe 2.57%
- Non-recovery 2.36%
- Moderate 15.51%
- Mild 36.41%
- Sub-threshold 43.16%

Source: Understanding Animal Research

The 10 organisations that carried out the most animal research in Great Britain in 2022

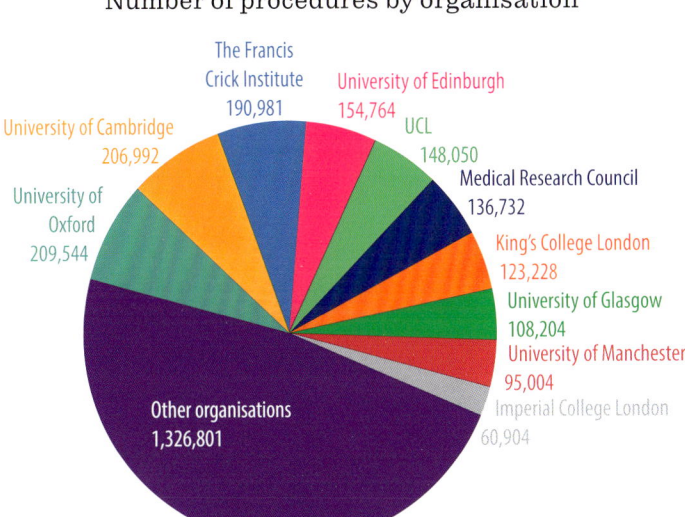

Each organisation proactively publishes these figures on their website. Animal research is operated under strict regulations put in place by the UK Home Office. All ten organisations are commited to open animal research communications.

Source: Understanding Animal Research

than once, that is 're- used', in certain circumstances. These instances are counted as separate, additional, procedures. As a result, the number of procedures is usually slightly higher than the number of animals used. 2,685,610 animals were used for the first time in 2022.

Specially protected species

Specially protected species refers to cats, dogs, horses, and non-human primates (monkeys) – they are subject to additional protection under Section 5C of the Animal (Scientific Procedures) Act 1986. This means these species can only be used when no other species is suitable. These species were used in 0.5% of all procedures.

Purpose of procedures

Procedures related to the creation and breeding of genetically altered (GA) animals decreased by 6% compared to 2021, while experimental procedures decreased by 12%.

Procedures for creation and breeding involve the breeding of animals whose genes have mutated or have been modified. These animals are used to produce genetically altered offspring for use in experimental procedures but are not themselves used in experimental procedures.

45% (1,248,994) of all procedures were for the creation or breeding of genetically altered animals.

Of these 1,248,994 procedures:

- 89% were for the purpose of maintenance of established lines of genetically altered animals.
- 11% were for the creation of new lines of genetically altered animals.

Experimental procedures involve using animals in scientific studies for purposes such as basic research and the development of treatments, safety testing of pharmaceuticals and other substances, education, specific surgical training and education, environmental research and species protection.

55% (1,512,210) of all procedures were for experimental purposes. This includes basic research, which expands our knowledge of living organisms and the environment; applied research, which addresses the prevention of disease and development of treatments; and regulatory research, which includes studies aimed at ensuring product safety and the effectiveness of pharmaceuticals. Of these 1,512,210 procedures:

- 53% were for basic research.
- 24% were for applied research.
- 22% were for regulatory research.
- 1% were for the protection of the natural environment, preservation of species, and higher education or training

The top three research areas for basic research were: the nervous system, immune system, and oncology. The top three research areas for applied research were: animal diseases and disorders, human cancer, and human infectious disorders. The top three research areas for regulatory research were: toxicity and other safety testing including pharmacology, quality control (batch safety testing), and routine production of blood-based products. Toxicity and other safety testing including pharmacology includes tests such as reproductive toxicity, developmental toxicity, and repeated dose toxicity (up to 28 days).

The use of animals to test tobacco products was banned in the UK in 1997 and it has been illegal to use animals to test cosmetic products in this country since 1998. A policy ban on household testing using animals was introduced in 2010. Since 2013, it has been illegal to sell or import cosmetics anywhere in the EU where the finished product or its ingredients have been tested on animals.

Severity of procedures

Severity assessments measure the harm experienced by an animal during a procedure. A procedure can be as mild as an injection, or as severe as an organ transplant.

Severity assessments reflect the peak severity of the entire procedure and are classified into five different categories:

Sub-threshold: When a procedure did not cause suffering above the threshold for regulation, that is, it was less than the level of pain, suffering, distress, or lasting harm that is caused by inserting a hypodermic needle according to good veterinary practice.

Non-recovery: When the entire procedure takes place under general anaesthetic and the animal is humanely killed before waking up.

Mild: Any pain or suffering experienced was only slight or transitory and minor so that the animal returns to its normal state within a short period of time. For example, the equivalent of an injection or having a blood sample taken.

Moderate: The procedure caused a significant and easily detectable disturbance to an animal's normal state, but this was not life-threatening. For example, surgery is carried out under general anaesthesia followed by painkillers during recovery.

Severe: The procedure caused a major departure from the animal's usual state of health and well-being. This would usually include long-term disease processes where assistance with normal activities such as feeding and drinking were required, or where significant deficits in behaviours/activities persist. Animals found dead are commonly classified as severe as pre-mortality suffering often cannot be assessed. Most severe procedures arise in regulatory testing such as the evaluation of the toxicity of drugs.

Why has the total number of procedures decreased this year?

The total number of animals used in research is affected by many factors. The overall funding for life sciences in the United Kingdom, as well as the relative funding in other countries, will change the amount of science done – a proportion of which will involve animals.

Animals are used alongside other techniques such as cell cultures, human studies and computational models. These methods are used – often in tandem – to answer the key biological questions necessary to understand and treat disease.

Animal research is strictly regulated in the UK. Every procedure, from a simple blood test to major surgery, requires individual, establishment and project licences, as well as approval from an Animal Welfare and Ethical Review Body. Before an animal is used, researchers must show that the knowledge could not be acquired using non-animal methods.

While the government produces these statistics on an annual basis, more organisations than ever before are openly publishing their own figures on their websites. This move towards greater transparency has been bolstered by the Concordat on Openness on Animal Research in the UK, which has been signed by 128 organisations since it launched in 2014.

Chris Magee, Head of Policy and Media, Understanding Animal Research, said:

'There was a drop of around 300,000 procedures this year, from just over 3 million to 2.76 million. Although roughly in accordance with long-term trends of declining animal use, year-on-year changes are primarily affected by the funding, focus and capacity of research teams.

That said, we would expect to see part of the decline as a result of new research methods being introduced to the lab that either don't use animals or use them differently, for instance being so mild that they no longer count as regulated procedures. Some new or improved non-animal methods also have the potential to give us better data, cheaper, and faster, although they are not a panacea and many will need support and development to be applied more widely.

New techniques are not confined to the non-animal space, as we've seen recently with transparent mice being used to successfully image tumours at unprecedented magnification and much earlier in the formation of the tumour than has previously been possible.

Thus, a focus on animal numbers masks a more exciting story of research innovation across the board with new animal models, improvements to old models, new approaches to research entirely and new synergies building between them. If the life sciences receives the support it needs to realise the full potential of these innovations then our scientific output, health and the environment can only benefit.'

13 July 2023

Super Summary

Choose five key facts from this article. Then write a short summary of the article.

The above information is reprinted with kind permission from Understanding Animal Research.
© 2024 Understanding Animal Research

www.understandinganimalresearch.org.uk

Where do Britons stand on animal testing?

A third support its use in medical products, but less than one in ten say the same for cosmetics.

By Connor Ibbetson

Singer Will Young handcuffed himself to the gates of a facility breeding dogs for laboratory experiments yesterday. This follows news from earlier in the year that a ruling from the EU could see animal testing for individual ingredients resumed in the UK for the first time since 1998.

The European Chemical Agency (ECA) ruled in August 2021 that a German firm, Symrise, would need to conduct animal tests on two ingredients used solely in cosmetics to comply with EU rules on chemicals. This ruling could mean animal testing would need to be carried out on 150 cosmetic ingredients used in the UK after the government said it would align with the ECA decision.

Under current UK law, the testing of completed cosmetics and their ingredients on animals is illegal, and it is also illegal to sell products that have been tested in this way. For medicines, the law states that potential completed medicines and their ingredients must be tested in animals before human trials can begin – albeit with stringent restrictions over how and when testing is performed.

A YouGov survey in August 2021 found that most Britons did not know the current law around animal testing of cosmetics, but were surer of the law around medical testing.

Only 34% correctly said that testing of cosmetic ingredients is illegal in the UK, while 37% didn't know and 29% incorrectly said it was legal. Similarly, 25% of people wrongly think animal testing of completed cosmetic products is legal in the UK, while 35% rightly said it was not. Another 40% were unsure.

Approaching half of people correctly said that the testing of individual medical ingredients (47%) and completed medicines (45%) are legal, with only 13% of people wrongly thinking both of these types of testing are illegal in the UK.

Do people support animal testing?

Despite it currently being not only legal, but a legal requirement, Britons tend to oppose animal testing of medicines. Around two-fifths say they oppose the testing of completed medicines (41%) and medical ingredients (44%) on animals. Around a third of people do support animal testing of therapeutics, however, including 37% in support of testing completed medical products and 35% in favour of testing their ingredients.

Approaching three-quarters of people (73%) are opposed to the testing of both ingredients and completed cosmetics on animals. This includes 58% of people 'strongly' opposed to both types of testing.

Current UK law does allow for some exceptions. Ingredients used in cosmetics can be tested on animals to examine environmental impact or worker safety – and only when there are no non-animal alternatives.

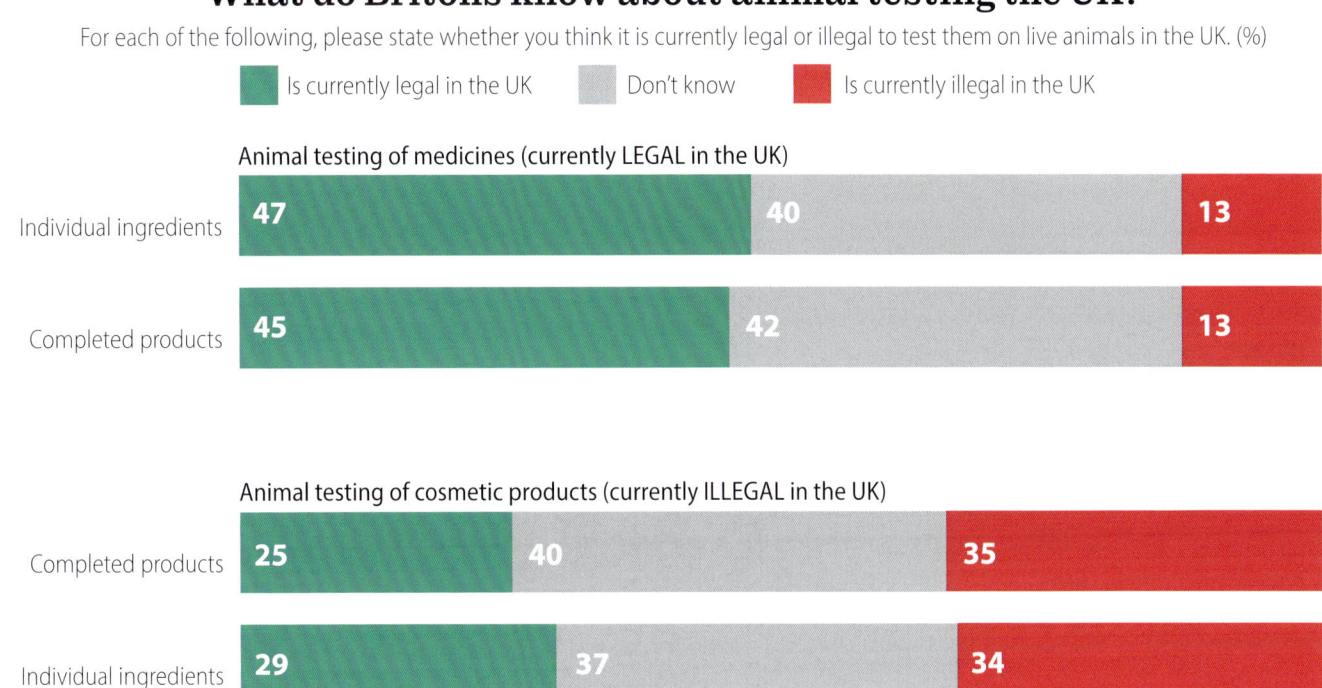

What do Britons know about animal testing the UK?
For each of the following, please state whether you think it is currently legal or illegal to test them on live animals in the UK. (%)

Is currently legal in the UK — Don't know — Is currently illegal in the UK

Animal testing of medicines (currently LEGAL in the UK)
- Individual ingredients: 47 / 40 / 13
- Completed products: 45 / 42 / 13

Animal testing of cosmetic products (currently ILLEGAL in the UK)
- Completed products: 25 / 40 / 35
- Individual ingredients: 29 / 37 / 34

Source: YouGov – 18-19 August 2021

Britons tend to oppose testing medicines on animals, and overwhelmingly oppose testing cosmetics on animals

Do you support or oppose companies being allowed to test the following on live animals? (%)

Source: YouGov – 18-19 August 2021

Is testing ingredients on animals acceptable if there is no alternative testing method?

Currently, testing individual ingredients on live animals can only be conducted in certain cases where there are no non-animal testing alternatives available.

Do you think animal testing of the following is or is not acceptable when there are no other testing methods available? (%)

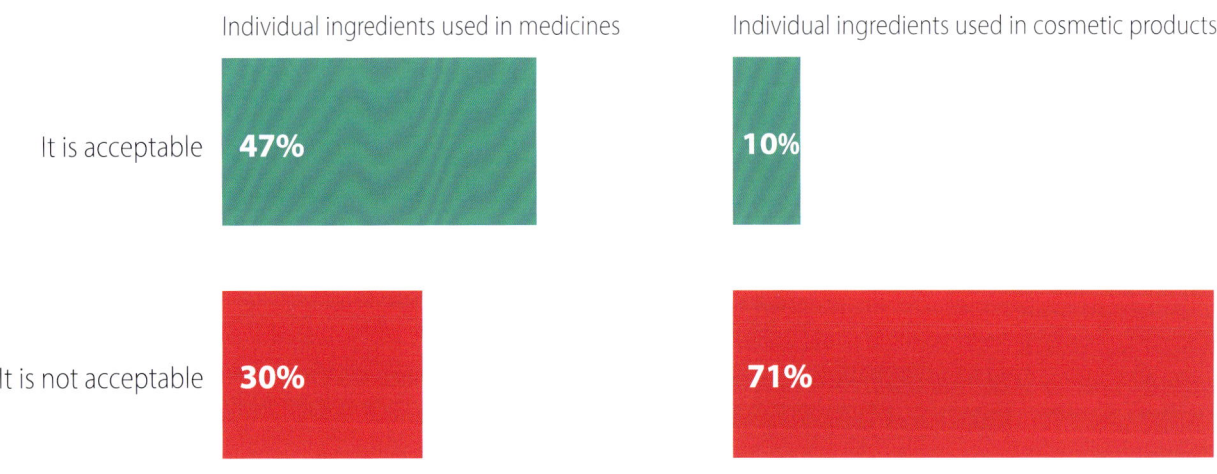

Source: YouGov – 18-19 August 2021

Some 47% of people think testing individual ingredients from medicines on animals is acceptable when there is no non-animal alternative, while 30% think it is not acceptable.

However, only 10% say it is acceptable to test cosmetic ingredients on animals even if there are no other tests available – the large majority (71%) think it is unacceptable.

17 November 2021

Research

Create your own survey to find out if your family and friends support or oppose animal testing. Is there any difference between age groups or genders?

The above information is reprinted with kind permission from YouGov.
© 2024 YouGov PLC

www.yougov.co.uk

Alternatives to animal testing: science, ethics and the law

Laura Rego Alvarez, Head of Science Policy and Regulation at Cruelty Free International, discusses the science and ethics behind alternatives to animal testing.

Animal testing remains a contentious topic in the science community and beyond. Some argue its benefits outweigh its ethical failures; others argue that it is morally wrong and, therefore, the practice should be stopped altogether.

Why do scientists test on animals?

A major reason why scientists continue to test on animals is the current way that hypotheses are tested in science. The process is one of testing models of increasing complexity with growing confidence in the hypothesis as it successfully passes each hurdle.

Therefore, the common justification for using animals is the apparent need to test a substance or idea in a 'complex, whole being' before there is enough confidence that it can be tested safely in humans. The assumption behind this is that the complex – that the whole being will capture all possible, unforeseen ways in which the substance or idea could be harmful (or not work), avoiding harm (or wasting time) to human volunteers. This 'complexity' argument is one reason for the lack of support for cell-based techniques, as these are seen as less complex and, therefore, inferior. This desire to capture all possible interactions appears to override the very real possibility that many of these interactions are the wrong ones by the very nature of testing in the wrong species. This is very frustrating for those that support non-animal approaches. There appears to be a real gap between the two groups regarding what is more important: complexity or relevance.

When it comes to animal-free research and testing, a chasm between what's possible and what's used exists for various reasons, including a lack of trust in less familiar methods, complicated and slow regulatory uptake, and inadequate funding.

Cruelty Free International maintains the Replace Animal Tests (RAT) List – a list of ten animal tests that still occur despite having widely accepted animal-free replacements, using an estimated 1.5 million animals each year in the EU alone. The RAT List highlights the fact that the existence of a non-animal replacement method isn't enough to secure its use – practical, social, and political factors must also be addressed.

Is animal testing our only option?

On top of the ethical question, testing on animals is neither our only option nor our best option. Due to the undeniable species differences between humans and animals, for example, major structural and physiological differences, data from animal tests cannot be a reliable basis for predicting the likelihood of specific effects in humans.

Even variations between humans make it difficult to extrapolate from one human sub-population to another. Therefore, the focus in medicine is shifting towards the individual patient, personalised medicine and the development of modern non-animal methods more directly applicable to human patients.

Alternatives to animal testing focus on human biology and use advanced cell-based and computational technologies to investigate diseases and potential treatments. These new methods, therefore, have the potential to deliver safer and more effective medicines more quickly and at less cost. Redirecting continued investment in failing animal experiments into human-specific medicine is urgently needed.

What are the alternatives to animal testing?

The last 30 years have seen a dramatic increase in alternatives to animal testing.

Non-animal methods include tissues and mini-organs grown in the laboratory from human cells, organs-on-chips (USB drive-sized devices that emulate human organs using cells connected by blood vessel-like channels), research conducted using human volunteers and advanced computer simulations.

These methods are already widely used in drug discovery and development because pharmaceutical companies recognise that they are more reliable and human-specific than animal tests. For example, a type of organ-on-a-chip known as a 'Liver-Chip' can detect drug-induced liver injury missed by animal tests.

Is animal testing effective?

The scientific process, being iterative, inevitably involves failure, but animal tests – due to two inherent weaknesses – far exceed this expected level of failure.

Firstly, tests on animals notoriously lack reliability, meaning that repeats of the same tests often produce conflicting results. Secondly – due to profound biological differences between humans and other animals, compounded by the sterile, standardised conditions of the laboratory – tests on animals frequently fail to predict human outcomes.

For example, 92% of medicines currently fail in human clinical trials even though they passed preclinical tests (including animal tests); 55% of failures are due to lack of efficacy, while 28% are due to toxic effects in humans. This general failure rate is bad enough, but failure is almost a certainty for drugs that treat complex and poorly understood conditions.

For instance, the failure rate of drugs intended to treat Alzheimer's disease is estimated to be higher than 99%. Only a handful (approximately 20) of novel medicines are released onto the market every year, and withdrawals and warnings of adverse effects commonly follow as the drug is tested in the wider population. This tells us that the animal testing paradigm, on which drug development remains largely based, is failing. The profound inefficiency of animal tests to predict safety and efficacy outcomes in humans, coupled with the huge cost (over $2 billion) and time (over a decade) required for new treatments to reach the market, is causing patients and society to suffer.

Why is animal testing unethical?

We believe there is no rational moral justification for using animals in experiments. Animals used in laboratories are deliberately harmed, not for their own good, and are usually killed at the end of the experiment.

Approximately three million experiments are conducted on sentient animals each year in the UK that, by their definition, cause pain, suffering, distress, or lasting harm. For example, animal experiments often involve: forcing animals to ingest or inhale potentially harmful substances or have them applied to their skin or injected into their bodies, surgically removing animals' organs or tissues to cause damage deliberately; or subjecting animals to frightening situations to create anxiety and depression.

Some experiments even require the animal to die as part of the test. For example, regulatory tests for Botox, vaccines and some tests for chemical safety are essentially variations of the cruel Lethal Dose 50 test in which 50% of the animals die or are killed just before the point of death.

Outside the tests, animals are usually confined to small, barren, unnatural enclosures that restrict natural behaviour and result in boredom and stress. Some animals in laboratories are confined on their own, without the companionship of others. Our investigations show time and time again that, despite claims by the animal research community, life inside a laboratory is no life at all.

What can individuals do to put a stop to animal testing?

Cruelty Free International works to achieve a world where no one wants or believes we need to test on animals, and we rely on the public globally to help us achieve that.

People in the UK can support our Target Zero campaign by contacting the Secretary of State for Business Energy and Industrial Strategy and their own Member of Parliament to call for an ambitious action plan to bring animal experiments to an end and a ministerial portfolio dedicated to making this happen.

EU residents can email the European Commission to ensure they listen to the results of our 'End Animal Testing' European Citizens' Initiative, signed by over 1.4 million people.

We are asking US residents to urge their Representative to become a cosponsor of three federal bills: the Humane and Existing Alternatives to Animals in Research and Testing Sciences (HEARTS) Act, which would prioritise the use and development of non-animal testing methods for generating new information on human biology and illness to deliver better medicines and healthcare products and protect the environment; the Companion Animal Release from Experiments (CARE) Act, which could ensure that animals are put up for adoption rather than killed when no longer wanted for experiments in laboratories that receive taxpayer funding from the National Institutes of Health; and the Humane Cosmetics Act, which would end animal testing for cosmetics in the US and stop the sale of new animal-tested cosmetics.

Caring consumers can choose to help end cosmetics animal testing by only buying from brands approved by our Leaping Bunny Programme. This allows consumers to choose their products, knowing that any Leaping Bunny approved brand has passed the most rigorous global criteria, which extend over and above laws governing animal testing.

What does the law say about animal testing?

While laws in place aim to protect animals in laboratories, they do not go far enough. Over the past decade, the number of animal tests in the UK has fallen by only 1% per year (discounting 2020's unusual drop due to the COVID-19 pandemic lockdowns).

If the UK continues its current trajectory, animal experiments will remain for at least another 90 years. We desperately need a strategy – including revision of the laws governing animal tests – that will put this country on a fast track to ending animal experiments completely.

5 December 2022

This piece was written and provided by Laura Rego Alvarez, Head of Science Policy and Regulation – Medicines, Cruelty Free International

The above information is reprinted with kind permission from Open Access Government.
© 2024 ADJACENT DIGITAL POLITICS LTD

www.openaccessgovernment.org

UK government confirms no legal requirement for animal testing in medical research

By Darcie Williams

In response to a recent question to the Department of Health and Social Care (DHSC), the UK government has categorically stated that animal testing in medical research is not a legal requirement.

This remarkable new response debunks the commonly held belief that animal testing is a legal requirement. Up until now, clarity on the government's position has been difficult to point to.

The written question, posed by MP Giles Watling – Chair of the All-Party Parliamentary Group on Animal Welfare – sought to understand whether the UK regulator considered approval of new therapies on a case-by-case basis, or whether they would always ask for a standard set of animal test results. Health Minister Will Quince affirmed in response that while there is no UK legislation mandating animal testing for this purpose, international regulatory guidelines are followed that suggest using animal data in the drug evaluation process.

So, what are these international regulatory guidelines that the UK follows exactly? They are a set of standards established by the International Council for Harmonisation of Technical Requirements for Pharmaceuticals for Human Use (ICH) – a body formed by the US, Europe, and Japan back in 1990. The ICH brings together regulators and members of the pharmaceutical industry to write guidelines on the development of medicines. The guidelines are then implemented by countries at a local level.

Within their guidelines, the ICH strongly suggests that a new drug should normally be tested on two species of animal (one rodent such as mice, and one non-rodent such as dogs or monkeys) before it can proceed to human clinical trials. However, in this recent response, the DHSC states that assessors will accept data from a 'suitably validated model that has been demonstrated to be predictive […] in lieu of animal data.' With this in mind, surely human-specific models such as organ-on-a-chip technology, which has proven to be more predictive than animal tests, could be submitted instead. This assertion of a more flexible approach from the government is entirely welcomed by those wishing to see progress for patients and animals.

And the UK can progress in this area because, critically, the ICH's guidelines are not legislation. This idea had previously been confirmed in evidence given to the All-Party Parliamentary Group (APPG) on Human Relevant Science by an employee of the Medicines and Healthcare Products Regulatory Agency (MHRA) in 2021. (Simply put, the MHRA regulates medicines in the UK, approving new drugs and ensuring they are safe to use and in good supply). The MHRA employee stated that 'there is no legal requirement that animal studies be used,' something that was backed-up by an expert in EU and international animal law at a subsequent meeting.

The same employee also confirmed that the MHRA accepted alternatives to animal studies, that animal studies should not be default, and that it made this clear to all sponsors of clinical trials. Up until this point, it had been difficult to clarify the MHRA's position on the requirement for animal tests. While the employee made it clear that they were speaking in a personal capacity, rather than officially representing the Agency, their evidence did provide confidence that the regulator is open to taking a more flexible and evidence-based approach.

In fact, we know that there is already a case in which the MHRA has been more progressive regarding the data it requires. In January 2019, the regulator approved in-human clinical trials for a cancer therapy developed by Achilles Therapeutics whose application had not been supported by animal data. The therapy involved using a patients' own immune cells to treat the cancer, rendering animal data particularly irrelevant.

In addition, development of the COVID-19 vaccines saw a global regulator depart from the usual requirement that animal tests must be completed before a therapy can move to human clinical trials. Specifically, the International Coalition of Medicines Regulatory Authorities (ICMRA) stated that 'it is not required to demonstrate the efficacy of the SARS- CoV-2 vaccine candidate in animal challenge models prior to proceeding to [first in-human] FIH clinical trials.' Moderna Therapeutics then carried out animal tests at the same time as human trials. Usually, the data from animal tests determines whether human trials go ahead, but in this instance, the two types of testing were carried out in parallel.

Around the world, policymakers are increasingly acknowledging the effectiveness of human-specific methodologies to get safer medicines to market quicker and more ethically.

Examples include the USA's Food and Drug Administration (FDA) Modernization Act 2.0 which explicitly states that it will accept data from human-specific sources in place of animal tests, and the European Parliament's 2021 resolution to phase out animal use by adopting an action plan. If it is to realise its vision of making the UK a Science Superpower, the UK Government must keep pace and take concrete policy action.

Nevertheless, while the response from the DHSC is a key development and cause for optimism, it is also important to note that animal tests that are carried out to satisfy such regulatory requirements make up only a small proportion of the animal experimentation that takes place in Britain – less than one-quarter in 2022, in fact. But of course, behind every statistic is an animal in a laboratory, and when broken down, the sheer number of animals that make up this portion is difficult to digest. In total last year, to satisfy the ICH guidelines, over 145,000 animals were used in experiments including over 86,000 mice, over 1,700 cynomolgus monkeys, and almost 2,500 beagles.

So, while we do now have more clarity on the government's current position in this area, it is important that we keep the pressure on policymakers to speed up the transition to human-specific, animal-free methodologies. Backing up this assertion with supportive action such as appointing a Minister for Human-Specific Technologies and developing an action plan will kickstart much-needed progress in this area.

Our vision is for a future where medical research breakthroughs are made using new technologies – not animals – and the government must play a central role in accelerating the UK's adoption of them. We hope that this is a sign that policymakers are listening.

13 November 2023

The above information is reprinted with kind permission from Animal Free Research UK
© 2010-2024 Animal Free Research UK

www.animalfreeresearchuk.org

Chapter 3

Animal Matters

Zoos repeatedly failing animals

Freedom for Animals has been campaigning for over 65 years for an end to keeping animals in zoos. Animals do not belong in captivity and there is sufficient evidence that many species, for example elephants, do not cope well with life in captivity. Captive elephants live shorter lives on average than wild living elephants, have poor reproductive success, high rate of stillbirth and infant mortality and significant foot, joint, and muscular problems.

Organisations like the British and Irish Association of Zoos and Aquariums (BIAZA) and the World Association of Zoos and Aquariums (WAZA) would have us believe that zoos are essential for conservation and education, yet over 60% of animals in zoos are not endangered in the wild and few, if any, zoo-bred animals are ever released back to the wild.

Zoos claim that they exist to educate people about the plight of wild animals around the world, yet even though zoos have existed for well over 100 years we are currently in a biodiversity crisis which would suggest that their education is not working. The overbreeding of animals in zoos results in many healthy animals being killed for having the wrong genes and therefore are surplus to zoos' breeding programmes. Zoos contribute very little to in situ conservation and even the biggest zoos commit less than 5% of their profits to real conservation. Not only do zoos fail wild animals generally by keeping them in captivity, but they also fail individual animals on a regular basis.

Every day seems to bring new reports of zoos failing animals. In the last week, three notable news articles from the UK popped up on social media news feeds:

Safari Park horror as Lioness killed almost instantly after being mauled by Lion

Edinburgh Zoo pandas to be replaced and sent back to China

The exciting changes being made at Chester Zoo in 2023

And just before Christmas, another three notable news articles popped up:

London Zoo welcomes new gorilla Kiburi just in time for Christmas

Longleat safari park red panda cubs die in cold snap

Rare tiger killed at Knowsley Safari during breeding attempt

There have been many more news articles throughout 2022 about animals dying, escaping, or behaving abnormally in zoos across the UK and indeed globally.

Individually these stories of animal suffering are dismissed by the zoo community as being unusual, rare occurrences and are not representative of zoos in general, but collectively these articles demonstrate a pattern of failure by zoos to adequately protect the animals in their care.

Longleat Safari Park

On New Year's Day an unnamed lioness was killed at Longleat Safari Park after being attacked by a male lion. This was witnessed by a visitor who alerted zoo staff who got to the enclosure as soon as they could, but the lioness was already dead. A zoo spokesperson said that such events are rare but 'naturally occur' – there is nothing natural about keeping animals in captivity in unnatural groups which individual lions did not choose to be in. This completely avoidable death came just a few weeks after two red pandas called Tala and Sumi froze to death at Longleat during a cold snap and less than two months after a female Amur tiger called Sinda was killed by a male tiger at Knowsley Safari

Park after the two had been forced together to try to get them to mate. The female suffered a fatal bite during the mating attempt. Again, a spokesperson for the zoo said that this was rare but 'natural.' However, this was also predictable and avoidable given that the male tiger had killed another female tiger in Copenhagen Zoo in 2018.

Edinburgh Zoo

It emerged earlier this week that two 19-year-old pandas, Tian Tian and Yang Guan, will be returned to China by Edinburgh Zoo after 12 years after the two failed to mate (at least seven failed attempts at artificial insemination) and provide the zoo with a baby panda to entice more paying visitors to visit. Prior to arriving at Edinburgh Zoo, the two had previously produced twins in China. Perhaps the stress of moving from China to Scotland impacted on their normal reproduction. It has also emerged that Edinburgh Zoo essentially rented the pandas for 10 years, extending to 12 years in 2021 for a fee of around £1,000,000 and may have spent as much as £20 million over 12 years. Treating wild animals such as these beautiful pandas as commodities to be hired to produce babies is simply unacceptable and not in the best interests of the animals. It is obvious that the zoo was not able to create an environment in which Tian Tian and Yang Guan could express their normal behaviours. The zoo even reduced the issue to a joke about whether the pandas would have swiped right on a well-known dating app. Not content with this failure, Edinburgh Zoo has announced that while it is sorry to be losing the pandas, they will be introducing a new 'exciting species' which will be announced in due course, thus condemning more wild animals to a life in captivity. In the meantime, to make as much money as possible from the pandas before they go back to China, Edinburgh Zoo is offering a Giant Panda Magic Moments Experience, where visitors can 'get closer than you ever imagined' helping the keepers feed the animals and a 'bespoke' VIP package – for just £5,000 (yes £5,000!), guaranteeing access to meet and feed the pandas (and four other species), along with a champagne breakfast. Does this sound like conservation or exploitation?

London Zoo

Just before Christmas a male western lowland gorilla called Kiburi was transported to London Zoo from Zoo Loro Parque in Tenerife (where they keep captive cetaceans who are forced to perform tricks for human entertainment), to replace a gorilla called Kumbuka who died in 2018. The story compared the Kiburi's journey to that of a Christmas present arriving in time for Christmas and zookeepers stated that they were hoping that Kiburi might get female gorillas Effie or Mjukuu under the mistletoe over the festive season. Treating such stories in such a light-hearted way is disrespectful to these sentient animals. The zoo stated that Kiburi would be part of an international breeding programme to protect populations of western lowland gorillas – however, there are currently estimated to be about 100,000 in the wild in western Africa and it is highly unlikely that any captive-bred gorillas will ever be returned to the wild. Instead, they will stay in captivity for their entire lives (up to 50 years in captivity). Ironically, just over a year ago, in November 2021, a leaked document revealed how a major zoo industry body had proposed the killing of gorillas in its member zoos. The proposal formed part of plans by the European Association of Zoos and Aquariums (EAZA) on how to deal with the 'overpopulation' of male western lowland gorillas, bred into captivity by zoos. EAZA has member zoos across Europe and West Asia who hold over 463 individual western lowland gorillas captive. 212 of these are male. Although EAZA said in 2021 that they had no immediate plans to kill any captive gorillas, it also confirmed that culling (that is killing) remains an option as part of the breeding programme. It does, however, raise the question of why zoos are continuing to breed western lowland gorillas if they already have too many and are considering killing unwanted, surplus gorillas.

Chester Zoo

Zoos – are they for conservation and education or simply tourist attractions aiming to maximise profits? Earlier this week the *Manchester Evening News* reported that Chester Zoo was planning some 'exciting' changes in 2023. The article said that the 'popular tourist attraction' (NB, not 'the popular conservation and education centre') would be introducing overnight accommodation, a new habitat, and to provide opportunities for wedding ceremonies, over the next few years. Unlikely to be exciting for the animals. How much will this cost, and wouldn't that money be better directed at in-situ conservation protecting wild animals and their habitats? Chester Zoo spends less than 5% on in-situ conservation. Most zoos don't spend as much as that. In 2019, Blackpool Zoo spent £5 million building a new elephant enclosure measuring just 0.01km^2 (2.4 acres), while in 2021 in the USA, Fort Worth Zoo in Texas spent $32 million (£23.6 million) on a new enclosure just 0.024km^2 (6 acres). Incredibly, Cincinnati Zoo has announced plans to spend $50 million (£36.9 million). Just think what these staggering sums of money could achieve for conservation of elephants in the wild.

The future

It's time to rethink wildlife conservation and bring an end to keeping wild animals in zoos. Zoos in the UK and around the world are failing animals – failing to provide appropriate environments which allow wild animals to express all their natural behaviours, failing to protect them from injury, failing to prevent them from escaping, risking their own well-being and that of the public, failing to prevent escapes, often with fatal consequences for the animals, but above all failing to deliver any conservation or education value. Zoos continue to over-breed animals even though some species are overpopulated in zoos leading to thousands of healthy animals being killed every year. Zoos continue to mutilate birds (pinioning) to prevent them from flying away. Too many failures and too many animals suffering as a result. Don't visit the zoo.

9 January 2023

The above information is reprinted with kind permission from Freedom for Animals.
© 2024 Captive Animals' Protection Society

www.freedomforanimals.org.uk

The animals that like visitors at the zoo – and those that want you to stay away

Elephants and bears enjoy people coming to say hello, but flightless birds and hedgehogs prefer to be left alone.

By Joe Pinkstone

Elephants might enjoy people saying hello to them in zoos, a study has suggested. Scientists believe elephants are happier around zoo visitors than alone in their paddocks, as various studies have found they become more social and less bored.

Cockatoos also seem to enjoy their fans and thrive when visitors come to see them, data showed – but hedgehogs and frogs prefer to be left alone.

Animal behaviour experts at Nottingham Trent University and Harper Adams University looked at more than 100 previous research papers exploring the various ways in which visitors impacted behaviour across more than 250 species in zoos.

The findings indicated that elephants in particular reacted positively to visitors.

According to the researchers, the repetitive behaviours that can indicate boredom also decreased in the presence of larger numbers of visitors.

The study also found that after public feedings, there was increased foraging by elephants and a decrease in their levels of inactivity.

Other species that displayed a positive response to visitors included penguins, jaguars, grizzly bears, polar bears, cheetahs, servals, banteng, and black-tailed prairie dogs.

And cockatoos may thrive from the stimulation of human visitors, another bird, the long-billed corella, spent the majority of time on busy days closer to the visitors.

Amphibians 'prefer humans to stay away'

More than half of the tests analysed in the review suggested animals are largely indifferent to the presence of humans. One type of animal in particular, however, seemed to prefer that humans stayed away.

'We reviewed the published literature on visitor effects on non-primates, and then looked at how animals responded,' explained Dr Ellen Williams, lead author for the study from Harper Adams University.

'Yes, there were some negative responses, but in terms of a species group level, the only animal type that showed negative responses more than chance were amphibians.

'That was however based on one paper though, and it was during COVID-19, so it's important not to read too much into it.' The impact of people on animals was largely negative but varied largely by species.

'The thing we really wanted to highlight was how variable the impact of visitors can be on non-primate species, as well as primate species. Visitors mean different things for different animals,' she told *The Telegraph*.

Animal groups for whom visitors were reported to have a negative impact included flightless birds, odd and even-toed ungulates, marsupials, ostriches, tuatara and hedgehogs.

Dr Samantha Ward, a zoo animal welfare scientist at Nottingham Trent University's School of Animal, Rural and Environmental Sciences, said: 'Some animal species have been born and raised in zoos and so have likely become used to the presence of humans,

'Zoo visitors are often aspects of a zoo animal's environment that animals cannot control and as such can be stressful, although some species appear to show good adaptability for the changing conditions of visitors,

'There can be a lot of variation in stimuli from visitors in terms of their behaviour, the noise they make and the way they interact with the animals,

'We have identified that species show varied responses to people in zoos – some cope well, others not so well.'

Dr Williams added: 'We have robust methods to measure animal welfare in zoos. Animal responses are attributed to various factors and recognising what these may be is important to improve welfare,

'In elephants and birds, it was encouraging to see a reduction in those repetitive behaviours towards something more positive in the presence of people, although the absence of change in the majority of species was also really good, because it suggests enclosure design is changing to better support animals in responding to visitors.'

The research was published in the journal *Animals*.

22 May 2023

The above information is reprinted with kind permission from *The Telegraph*.
© Telegraph Media Group Limited 2024

www.telegraph.co.uk

The horrors behind wearing fur, skin and feathers

Fashion serves as a powerful channel for self-expression but sadly, many people remain unaware of the suffering and harsh cruelty associated with some brands.

By Rebecca Grove

Every year, countless wild animals face exploitation and the grim fate of being sacrificed for the gains of fashion labels that lag behind in embracing advanced and compassionate fashion alternatives.

Within the fur trade, for example, animals such as foxes and mink are forced into a life of captivity before they meet their end while crocodiles and various other reptiles face a horrific fate for the sake of obtaining 'exotic skins.' Majestic birds like ostriches are killed for both their feathers and hides.

With events like London Fashion Week happening, we've put together a list that shows the dark side of the fashion industry.

Choosing fur is choosing cruelty

The methods of slaughter on fur factory farms prioritise profit by protecting the integrity of full skins.

Whether trapped or shot in the wild, or confined in barren cages until their slaughter, there is no way to transform a wild animal into a coat, bag, or shoe without immense cruelty and suffering in the process.

Did you know…

- Around 100 million animals are killed each year globally in the fur trade.
- The wild animal species most commonly exploited and slaughtered for their fur include mink, foxes, chinchillas and raccoon dogs.
- Animals on fur farms are kept in small cages and suffer severe psychological distress in a system unable to ever meet their needs.
- The methods of slaughter on fur factory farms prioritise profit by protecting the integrity of full skins.

Smaller animals like mink are killed by gas, while those slightly larger animals like foxes and raccoon dogs are electrocuted.

The dark truth behind the skin trade

Crocodiles are cruelly slaughtered at two-to-three-years-old, despite a natural average lifespan of 70 years.

Snakes, lizards, alligators, and various crocodile species all fall victim to exploitation and slaughter for the fashion industry. Among them, Crocodylus porosus, the saltwater crocodile, is one of the most sought-after skins in the world of luxury fashion.

Did you know…

- *Crocodylus porosus* skin is so popular due to its rigid, scaled texture and length. Bags and other items made from it can be sold for hundreds of thousands of dollars.
- Australian factory farms provide 60% of the global trade in saltwater crocodile skins.
- While crocodiles are often offered somewhat more space than the minimum requirement, they are caged so tightly that they are unable to turn around in many instances.
- Crocodiles are slaughtered at two to three years old, despite a natural average lifespan of 70 years.

Feathers are for birds, not for fashion

Ostriches do not have a moulting season, and so their feathers are either plucked or cut off.

Ostriches are the primary source of exotic feathers most frequently employed in today's fashion industry.

Did you know…

- On a farm, ostriches are often packed tightly together, fed lucerne in a controlled system where they are unable to act out natural behaviours.
- Unlike many other birds, ostriches do not have a moulting season, and so their feathers are either plucked or cut off.
- Ostrich skins are also highly coveted by the fashion industry, because of the raised, circular marks on ostrich skin from where their feathers have been plucked.
- Before ostriches are slaughtered, they can be denied food for 24 hours under Australian and South African codes of practice.

20 September 2023

The above information is reprinted with kind permission from World Animal Protection.
© 2024 World Animal Protection

www.worldanimalprotection.org

Why would anyone shoot an elephant for fun?

Every year, trophy hunters slaughter tens of thousands of wild animals, bizarrely claiming that killing rare species is an effective way to protect them. Born Free's Head of Policy, veterinarian Dr Mark Jones, reports.

Trophy hunting is the killing of selected wild animals for sport or pleasure, by predominantly wealthy Westerners, and it is a big business. Hunters pay huge sums to kill wild animals, then post pictures of themselves next to the dead bodies of their victims, before displaying the animals' heads, skins, or other body parts on their walls or trophy cabinets.

Born Free has campaigned to end the grotesque, so-called 'sport' of trophy hunting since our inception. We strongly refute claims that trophy hunting significantly supports conservation or local communities, and are currently raising funds to fight elephant exploitation and protect elephants in the wild.

Every year tens of thousands of wild animals are brutally killed by trophy hunters. Among them are hundreds of elephants in southern Africa. The individual elephants who are targeted for this so-called 'sport' suffer immensely at the hands of the hunters. Many have to be chased and shot multiple times before they finally succumb.

But it's not just the individuals who suffer. The trophy hunters say they target 'redundant' or 'problem' animals, and that their fees pay for conservation efforts. But the reality is that elephants are highly intelligent, socially complex animals, and no elephant is 'redundant' in their complex society. The killing of elephants can disrupt herds and lead to increased conflict between elephants and people, with more victims on both sides.

In April 2022, we learned that two 'big tuskers' – older male elephants whose tusks weigh upwards of 50kg and may reach the ground – had been killed by foreign trophy hunters in a remote corner of Botswana. There may be as few as 20 big tuskers left in the wild across Africa. Their knowledge and experience are irreplaceable.

Elephant populations across Africa have already been devastated through habitat loss and poaching. By cruelly taking out important members of their remaining social groups, trophy hunters are only making matters worse.

Elephants also have a dramatic impact on the wider ecology through their role as the 'gardeners of the forest,' dispersing seeds and creating habitats for a myriad of other species. The activities of forest elephants have been shown to increase the ability of forest ecosystems to sequester carbon. The unnecessary and premature loss of even one elephant damages this potential.

As a vet, a keen naturalist and a student of animal behaviour, elephants fascinate me. They display traits such as empathy and compassion, they care for each other's young, and they communicate over long distances, traits we tend to think are exclusive to us humans.

The desire among trophy hunters to pay to kill these and other animals is something I am at a complete loss to understand.

Born Free is ethically opposed to the hunting or killing of any animal for sport or pleasure. We also challenge the claims made by proponents of trophy hunting that it delivers significant conservation and community benefits, or that it positively contributes to the sustainable use of wildlife. We strive to highlight to policymakers and the public, the negative impacts of trophy and sport hunting activities on the welfare and conservation of animals.

You can help us by calling on the government in the UK to make good on its promise to ban the imports of hunting trophies from elephants and other threatened and protected species. It may not bring an immediate end to trophy hunting, but it will send a clear message that, as a society, we believe it should be consigned to history where it belongs.

22 November 2023

The above information is reprinted with kind permission from Born Free.
© 2024 Born Free/www.bornfree.org.uk

www.bornfree.org.uk

There's no such thing as an 'overbred' dog – here's why

There's no such thing as an 'overbred dog' since all breeding is overbreeding. With more than 70 million homeless animals struggling to survive on any given day in the US, there is no excuse for bringing any additional animals into the world. Plus, all purebred dogs are prone to suffering from health problems. When those unhealthy purebred dogs are described as the 'most popular' breeds, greedy breeders bring more and more of them into the world to make a profit. What breeders and the 'pet' industry typically won't mention is the lifetime of suffering that these overbred dogs will be forced to endure.

The top 10 'overbred' dogs and their ailments

1. French Bulldog

After a French Bulldog named Winston won Best in Show at the 2022 National Dog Show, a new statistic by the American Kennel Club (AKC) – a purebred dog registry – revealed that the breathing-impaired breed was the most registered breed in 2022.

In addition to brachycephalic airway syndrome, which makes breathing nearly impossible, French bulldogs suffer from the following:

- Cataracts
- Cleft lip/palate
- Corkscrew tail (deformed vertebrae)
- Corneal ulcers
- Dystocia (difficulty giving birth)
- Ear infections
- Elbow dysplasia
- Entropion (eyelid disorder)
- Haemophilia (blood disease)
- Hemivertebra (spinal deformity)
- Inflammatory bowel disease
- Intervertebral disc disease
- Patellar luxation
- Prolapsed nictitating membrane gland (cherry eye)
- Skin infections
- Upper respiratory tract disorders.

2. Labrador Retriever

Until 2023, Labrador Retrievers had been the most AKC-registered dog breed for 31 years.

Over the course of those three decades, Labrador Retrievers were shown to have suffered from the following:

- Cataracts
- Corneal dystrophy
- Cranial cruciate ligament rupture
- Ear infections
- Entropion and ectropion (eyelid problems)
- Epilepsy
- Gastric dilatation and volvulus (bloat) and other gastrointestinal problems
- Hereditary myopathy (muscular disorder)
- Hip and elbow dysplasia
- Neoplastic disorders, including cancer
- Neuroaxonal dystrophy (neurological disorder)
- Obesity
- Osteoarthritis or degenerative joint disease

- Panosteitis (inflammation of the bone marrow)
- Progressive retinal atrophy
- Skeletal dwarfism
- Skin disorders.

3. Bulldog

The medical conditions afflicting Bulldogs are so severe that Norway banned the breeding of British Bulldogs after a court there ruled that the dogs could never be considered healthy, in large part because of their status as a breathing-impaired breed. As a result of selective breeding, Bulldogs (also known as 'British Bulldogs' or 'English Bulldogs') can often only breed via artificial insemination and caesarean section because their heads are too large and their hips too small to give birth naturally. They also commonly suffer from breathing problems and the following conditions:

- Conjunctivitis
- Corkscrew tail (tail deformity)
- Demodectic mange
- Dermatitis
- Entropion (eyelid problem)

- Heart problems
- Heat and exercise intolerance
- Hemivertebra (spinal deformity)
- Prolapsed nictitating membrane gland (cherry eye)
- Upper and lower respiratory tract disorders.

4. Golden Retriever

Golden Retrievers are at a higher risk than most other breeds of suffering from:

- Cervical vertebral instability (wobbler syndrome)
- Dermatitis
- Diabetes
- Elbow and hip dysplasia
- Entropion (eyelid problem)
- Heart conditions (multiple types)
- Hypothyroidism
- Idiopathic epilepsy
- Kidney dysplasia
- Muscular dystrophy
- Portosystemic shunt (deformity affecting the liver)
- Progressive retinal atrophy
- Retinal dysplasia
- Von Willebrand's disease (bleeding disorder).

5. German Shepherd

German Shepherds often have genetic predispositions to the following:

- Cervical vertebral instability (wobbler syndrome)
- Cutaneous asthenia (Ehlers-Danlos syndrome)
- Degenerative lumbosacral stenosis (narrowing of the posterior spinal canal)
- Degenerative myelopathy (progressive, incurable disease of the spinal cord)
- Epilepsy (idiopathic)

- Exocrine pancreatic insufficiency (inadequate production of digestive enzymes)
- Familial cutaneous vasculopathy (blood vessel disorder leading to skin abnormalities)
- Footpad disorder
- Gastric dilatation and volvulus (bloat)
- Heart conditions (multiple types)
- Hemivertebra (spinal deformity)
- Hip and elbow dysplasia
- Hyperadrenocorticism (Cushing's disease)
- Megaesophagus
- Myasthenia gravis (neuromuscular disorder)
- Panosteitis (inflammation of the bone marrow)
- Platelet procoagulant deficiency (blood disorder)
- Progressive retinal atrophy
- Pyoderma (bacterial skin infection)
- Retinal dysplasia
- Von Willebrand's disease (blood disorder).

6. Pug

Because pugs are a breathing-impaired breed, they are 54 times more likely to suffer from brachycephalic obstructive airway syndrome – a condition that greatly limits their ability to breathe – than other types of dogs. They're also at higher risk of suffering from the following issues, among many others:

- Diabetes
- Exercise intolerance
- Encephalitis (brain inflammation), including necrotising meningo-encephalitis
- Joint dislocation
- Keratoconjunctivitis sicca (dry eyes)
- Obesity
- Proptosis (bulging eyes)

- Skin disorders, including demodectic mange
- Spinal deformities, including spina bifida and hemivertebra.

7. Cavalier King Charles Spaniel

These Spaniels have been bred to have unnaturally shaped skulls, which can cause a condition called syringomyelia, in which the skull is too small for the brain, forcing brain tissue to protrude through the base of the skull and put pressure on the spinal cord. It's estimated that more than 90% of Cavalier King Charles Spaniels suffer from this extremely painful disease. These spaniels are also likely to suffer from several other health problems, including these:

- Brachycephalic obstructive airway syndrome
- Diabetes
- Ear infections
- Epilepsy
- Hip dysplasia
- Ichthyosis (fish scale disease)
- Keratoconjunctivitis sicca (dry eye)
- Microphthalmia (abnormally small eyes)
- Mitral valve disease
- Patellar luxation
- Progressive retinal atrophy.

8. Beagle

Beagles face an elevated risk of developing health problems, including these:

- Cataracts
- Cervical vertebral instability (wobbler syndrome)
- Deafness
- Demodectic mange
- Epilepsy
- Glaucoma
- Hypothyroidism

- Intervertebral disc disease
- Progressive retinal atrophy
- Prolapsed nictitating membrane gland (cherry eye)
- Retinal dysplasia.

9. Boxer

According to research compiled by the Royal Veterinary College in London, boxers are genetically predisposed to 76 different health conditions. These are some of their most common ailments:

- Cervical vertebral instability (wobbler syndrome)
- Corneal dystrophy
- Cutaneous asthenia (Ehlers-Danlos syndrome)
- Degenerative myelopathy
- Demodectic mange
- Eye ulcers
- Gastric dilatation and volvulus (bloat)
- Heart conditions (multiple, including dilated cardiomyopathy)
- Hip dysplasia
- Hyperadrenocorticism (Cushing's disease)
- Hypothyroidism
- Inflammatory bowel disease
- Mast cell tumour (malignant cancer of white blood cells involved in immunity)
- Progressive retinal atrophy.

10. Dachshund

Dachshunds face a host of health problems. Their long backs and short legs lead to a higher risk of lifelong spinal, knee, and other joint problems. They are also particularly susceptible to these issues:

- Blood disorders, including Von Willebrand's disease and pyruvate kinase deficiency
- Cataracts
- Corneal dystrophy
- Deafness
- Elbow dysplasia
- Epilepsy
- Glaucoma
- Hyperadrenocorticism (Cushing's disease)
- Immune-mediated thrombocytopenia (blood disorder)
- Intervertebral disc disease
- Microphthalmia (abnormally small eyes)
- Progressive retinal atrophy
- Skin conditions, including demodectic mange.

What is the true cost of purchasing a dog?

Buying a purebred dog supports breeding, and breeding produces dogs who often suffer from painful health problems throughout their lives. Buying a purebred also takes a potential home away from a dog in a shelter. Don't throw money at the dog-breeding industry, which clearly doesn't care about animals' well-being. There are millions of dogs in need of loving homes, so adopt from a shelter if you're ready to make a lifetime commitment.

26 June 2023

Courtesy of People for the Ethical Treatment of Animals (PETA).
The above information is reprinted with kind permission from PETA.
© 2024 PETA

www.peta.org

Puppy smuggling crackdown and live exports ban dropped in major government U-turn

Rishi Sunak, who promised last year to champion Kept Animals Bill, accused of breaking promises in Tory manifesto.

By Jane Dalton

The government has dropped plans for a bill that would have banned live exports and cracked down on puppy smuggling, prompting waves of fury from animal welfare campaigners and experts.

The Kept Animals Bill – which also included a ban on primates as pets, a crackdown on puppy smuggling and greater protection for sheep from dangerous dogs – was in the Conservatives' election manifesto.

The promises were mainstays of the government's 2021 grand animal welfare action plan, and the Bill was one of Boris Johnson's flagship policies.

During his Tory leadership campaign last year, Rishi Sunak promised to ban live animal exports and to champion the Kept Animals Bill.

When the heads of nearly 30 campaign organisations called on him and rival Liz Truss to promise to uphold the pledges, Mr Sunak's team replied saying: 'Rishi looks forward to championing this bill as it continues to progress through Parliament'

The legislation would also have tackled pet theft, improved rules on zoo animal welfare and banned the import of dogs with cropped ears.

Environment, Food and Rural Affairs Minister Mark Spencer announced on Thursday the government was dropping it, citing a lack of parliamentary time – but sources said the government feared it could lead to debates over the hunting ban.

Animal welfare campaigners accused the prime minister of breaking Tory promises.

Claire Bass, Senior Director of Campaigns and Public Affairs at Humane Society International/UK, said: 'The government's decision to abandon the Kept Animals Bill is an astonishing betrayal of both animals and public trust.'

She said the bill needed only a few more hours in the Commons to succeed, so parliamentary time clearly was not the real issue.

She said Whitehall sources had said the bill had been dropped over concerns it could 'act as a vehicle for uncomfortable debates that the government does not want held on polarising issues such as hunting with dogs.'

Hunting wild mammals with dogs is illegal under the Hunting Act 2004.

'Vital protections for dogs, calves, sheep, primates, and other animals have been sacrificed today at the government's altar of self-serving political convenience,' Ms Bass said.

Battersea, Blue Cross, Cats Protection, Dogs Trust, Royal Society for the Prevention of Cruelty to Animals (RSPCA) and The Kennel Club joined forces to condemn the U-turn, saying animals 'will now continue to suffer without the protections the bill could have provided, including victims of puppy and kitten smuggling, dog and cat abduction and the importation of dogs with cropped ears and declawed cats.'

Before Brexit, an estimated 4,000 sheep were transported from the UK to Europe for slaughter each year, and around

6,000 calves were exported from Scotland via Northern Ireland, mostly to Spain and Italy. Exports from Northern Ireland continue.

The government had come under pressure to move ahead with the bill, which had been stalled since its report stage in the Commons.

British Veterinary Association President Malcolm Morley said: 'News that the Kept Animals Bill will not progress through Parliament is extremely disappointing. This crucial legislation, and the package of measures it contained, would have prevented the immeasurable suffering of thousands of animals.'

The RSPCA said it was frustrated and disappointed that, despite overwhelming public support, the government had 'delayed and delayed' and had now broken up the bill.

Emma Slawinski, Head of Policy at the RSPCA, said: 'We have been waiting for almost two years for the Kept Animals Bill to improve the lives of billions of animals and now it's effectively been scrapped. While politicians dither, animals suffer.'

Mr Spencer suggested the measures could be brought into law through Private Members' Bills – but such bills rarely make it through Parliament.

Nick Palmer, Head of Compassion in World Farming UK, said: 'This cruel and outdated trade has been a stain on British farm animal welfare standards for far too long, and the Kept Animals Bill would have finally consigned it to the history books. But sadly, the government have let this opportunity slide.

'We urge MPs who are successful in the ballot for Private Members' Bills in the autumn, to take up the ban and propose legislation to finally end this horrific practice which has caused so much suffering over the years.'

Ms Bass said the U-turn was 'indicative of the low priority the government now evidently places on animal welfare.'

Other animal lovers branded the decision 'shameful', and one commented: 'The UK is supposed to be one of the leaders in animal welfare. What a joke that is, especially where the Tory government is concerned.'

Mr Spencer told MPs: 'We will be taking forward measures in the Kept Animals Bill individually during the remainder of the Parliament,

'We remain fully committed to delivering our manifesto commitments – and this approach is now the surest and the quickest way of doing so, rather than letting it be mired in political game-playing.'

The Independent has asked No. 10 to comment on the U-turn in the light of Mr Sunak's promise last year, but has not received a response.

26 May 2023

Research

In small groups, research stories of puppy/kitten smuggling, or animal theft. Have a look at the story. Why do you think that it happened? What measures could be put in place to prevent it from happening again?

Write

Write a persuasive letter to your MP to reconsider the The Kept Animals Bill. Give your reasons why the bill should be introduced and provide some facts to reinforce your argument.

Key Facts

- Hunting wild mammals with dogs is illegal under the Hunting Act 2004.
- Before Brexit, an estimated 4,000 sheep were transported from the UK to Europe for slaughter each year, and around 6,000 calves were exported from Scotland via Northern Ireland, mostly to Spain and Italy.

The above information is reprinted with kind permission from *The Independent*.
© independent.co.uk 2024

www.independent.co.uk

Dogs being killed, poisoned, beaten, and mutilated on massive scale, says RSPCA

Cost-of-living crisis and pandemic created animal welfare crisis, says charity as cruelty cases climb 20% in a year.

By Jane Dalton

Dogs are being killed, poisoned, beaten and mutilated on a 'massive scale' – and attacks are rising, the RSPCA says.

Cases of deliberate harm to dogs, including improper and attempted killings, have increased by more than a quarter – 27% – in three years, which the charity thinks could be down to financial strains on owners.

Last year, the RSPCA received 9,776 reports of dog cruelty in England, compared with 8,176 in 2021 and 7,691 in 2020.

The number equates to 27 dogs a day being cruelly treated – more than one every hour – and a rise of nearly 20%.

Dermot Murphy, head of the RSPCA's rescue officers, said: 'Right now, animal cruelty is happening in England and Wales on a massive scale and rising.

'It's heartbreaking that we are seeing such sad figures, which show animal cruelty is on the rise.

'While we don't know for certain why there has been an increase, the cost-of-living crisis and the post-pandemic world have created an animal welfare crisis.'

Overall, 42,690 reports were made last year to the charity about dogs – including intentional harm, neglect and abandonments – a seven% increase in a year.

Beatings of animals accounted for more than three in four cruelty complaints, rising by 22% to 9,658.

Such reports peaked in August 2022, when 1,081 were received – an average of 35 a day – in line with a pattern of cruelty regularly increasing in summer.

In 2021, a puppy called Terry was left with life-threatening head injuries after his then-owner beat him until he collapsed, lifeless.

A member of the public rushed the Whippet to Hull People's Dispensary for Sick Animals (PDSA) pet hospital, where staff believed he was already dead until they noticed light breathing and saved his life.

Vet nurse Rachel Coombes, who helped in the emergency treatment and eventually adopted the puppy, said: 'I just felt a connection as soon as he was brought in as he was in such a state we actually thought initially he hadn't made it,

'Then when we spotted gentle breathing, I said, "If he survives this I am going to give him a home" which is exactly what I did.'

Mr Murphy said: 'Dogs are the most abused animal in this country and we investigate more complaints about them than any other type of animal.'

The skinniest dog a rescuer had ever seen in his 16-year career with the RSPCA was found barely alive dumped in a street in South Yorkshire.

The animal had lost 98% of its fur due to an untreated skin condition and had a broken tailbone so badly infected that part of it had rotted off.

Before being rescued, the Greyhound/Lurcher-cross was so weak it could barely move.

RSPCA figures also show the number of animals killed in 'suspicious circumstances' climbed by 15% in 12 months, to 891 last year.

Last month, the charity revealed cat cruelty rose by 25% last year, leaving five cats a day suffering at the hands of humans.

Reports to the charity about intentional harm to cats reached 1,726 – up from 1,387 in 2021.

Sam Gaines, head of the RSPCA's companion animal department, said: 'In many cases, these pets have been injured deliberately by their owners, the very people who are supposed to love and protect them,

'But cats are also more vulnerable as they tend to be out and about on their own, which can leave them vulnerable to airgun attacks and other forms of cruelty by complete strangers.'

The charity's Cancel Out Cruelty campaign raises funds for rescue teams.

25 August 2023

Key Facts

- In 2022, the RSPCA received 9,776 reports of dog cruelty in England, compared with 8,176 in 2021 and 7,691 in 2020.
- 27 dogs experience cruelty each day, compared to 5 cats.
- in 2022, 42,690 reports were made to the RSPCA about dogs.
- RSPCA figures show the number of animals killed in 'suspicious circumstances' climbed by 15% in 12 months, to 891 in 2022.

The above information is reprinted with kind permission from *The Independent*.
© independent.co.uk 2024

www.independent.co.uk

Should we keep animals as pets?

Pets are often seen as a source of love, comfort and companionship. They become loyal friends, members of the family and even service animals. In the United Kingdom, approximately 12 million households keep pets. However, the question of their ethical treatment has always been a topic of debate. Is it right to keep animals as pets?

Firstly, people argue that pets bring joy and happiness to their owners. They can help reduce stress, prevent loneliness, and provide comfort to those with mental health issues. In addition, many people believe that pets help teach children important life lessons and develop empathy. Pets can encourage responsibility, such as getting children to feed and look after them. Moreover, they teach children how to handle relationships, to respect other living beings, and encourage physical exercise through active playtime. This means that pets have a positive impact on the mental and physical development of children.

Despite the positive aspects of pet ownership, many people believe that it is unethical to keep animals as pets. Firstly, some pets are taken from their natural habitat and transported to different countries where they then face new and unfamiliar environments and climates. This can be traumatic for them and cause significant stress. Moreover, animals that are bred in captivity have been removed from their natural environment. They may not adapt well to their new surroundings, and may not be able to develop the skills they would have had in the wild. This includes their natural instincts, and the ability to hunt for their food or interact with animals from their species.

In addition, some animals are bred for their physical appearance, rather than for their health and well-being. This includes dogs with shorter snouts, which can cause breathing problems and other health issues. Breeding practices also lead to overpopulation, and there are thousands of unwanted pets looking for a home in shelters.

Another issue associated with pets is the behaviour of pet owners. Many pet owners do not understand the needs of their pets and do not provide them with the care and attention they need. This can lead to malnourishment, illness, and abuse. Not giving pets proper attention can cause them to become lonely, bored, and isolated. In worse cases, mistreating them has caused physical harm, which brings about emotional distress to the pets.

In conclusion, owning a pet has both positive and negative aspects, and the ethical question of whether or not it is right to keep animals as pets will continue to be debated. What is important is that we recognise the rights of animals, and provide them with an environment that is suitable for their well-being. It is essential to balance the pet's welfare, its owner's lifestyle, and safety concerns.

So, what do you think? Should we keep animals as pets?

Debate

As a class, debate the question 'Is it ethical to keep animals as pets?'. Half of the class will be for keeping pets, and the other half against.

Further Reading/Useful Websites

Useful websites

www.animalfreeresearchuk.org

www.animaljusticeproject.com

www.bornfree.org.uk

www.crueltyfreeinternational.org

www.freedomforanimals.org.uk

www.independent.co.uk

www.openaccessgovernment.org

www.peta.org

www.telegraph.co.uk

www.theconversation.com

www.theguardian.com

www.thehumaneleague.org.uk

www.understandinganimalresearch.org.uk

www.worldanimalprotection.org

www.worldanimalprotection.org

www.yougov.co.uk

References
pages: 12-13
1. https://www.peta.org.uk/issues/animals-not-experiment-on/cosmetics/
2. https://www.hsi.org/news-resources/about/
3. https://www.hsi.org/news-resources/as-south-korea-contemplates-a-dog-meat-ban-charity-closes-its-18th-dog-meat-farm-and-flies-dogs-to-united-states-to-seek-adoption/
4. https://www.hsi.org/news-resources/save-ralf-koreans-to-support-alternatives-to-animal-testing-law/
5. https://chemicalwatch.com/201777/south-korea-proposes-law-to-promote-alternatives-to-animal-testing
6. https://www.hsi.org/news-resources/hsi-korea-welcomes-historic-bill-to-prioritize-technologies-that-replace-animal-testing-in-south-korea/
7. https://www.hsi.org/news-resources/petition-for-swift-passage-of-bill-to-replace-animal-testing-is-delivered-to-south-koreas-national-assembly/
8. https://www.hsi.org/news-resources/south-korea-to-end-unnecessary-animal-test/
9. https://koreajoongangdaily.joins.com/2022/05/29/culture/features/kor

Further Reading
Are We Smart Enough to Know How Smart Animals Are? by Frans de Waal (Granta, £10.99)
Other Minds: The Octopus and the Evolution of Intelligent Life by Peter Godfrey-Smith (William Collins, £9.99)
Sentient: What Animals Reveal About Our Senses by Jackie Higgins (Picador, £20)
The Book of Minds by Philip Ball

Glossary

Animal research
The process of using animals in scientific research. Also called 'animal experimentation' or 'animal testing'. Animal research for the purposes of testing cosmetic products is largely banned in the European Union. However, the use of animals in research and testing for medical purposes is still considered essential by the majority of the scientific community.

Animal rights
This term usually refers to the view that animals should be respected and treated in the same way as human beings. Animal rights campaigners reject the treatment of animals as property and campaign for their recognition as legal beings.

Animal rights extremists
Animal rights extremists object to the exploitation of animals by human beings, and in recent years their particular focus has been the use of animals in medical tests by pharmaceutical companies. Extremists have been known to use tactics including death threats, planting bombs and destroying property against pharmaceutical workers and their families.

Animal stunning
While the purpose of stunning is to make an animal unconscious by electrocuting it, as opposed to killing it straight away, some methods of stunning may induce heart attacks. Head-only electrical stunning can induce unconsciousness without stopping the heart from beating, and this means that the animal is still alive when the throat is cut.

Animal Welfare Act 2006
Passed in 2006, this animal welfare legislation came into force in 2007. While it largely repealed and replaced the 1911 Protection of Animals Act, the law also made it an offence to fail to ensure the welfare of an animal, and to dock the whole, or any part, of a dog's tail. Anyone found guilty of committing offences could be banned from owning animals, fined up to £20,000 and/or given a prison sentence.

Cloning
The asexual reproduction of identical copies of an original. Cloning is an extremely controversial area of scientific research – human cloning, and to a lesser extent animal cloning, for reproductive purposes has caused considerable concern with the public.

Conservation
Safeguarding biodiversity; attempting to protect endangered species and their habitats from destruction.

Fake fur (faux fur)
First introduced in 1929, fake fur mimics the appearance and feel of fur. Often made of plastic, fake fur can be detrimental to the environment.

Furrier
Furrier's are skilled craftsmen and women who use animal fur in order to produce fur garments.

Hunting
Hunting is the killing of animals for food or sport. It includes trophy hunting, where people kill animals and keep and display their body parts.

Invertebrates
Invertebrates is a term which describes animals without a backbone, and is used to refer to insects, shellfish, octopuses, snails and other animals.

Personhood
The state of being a person, which in turn entitles them to have basic legal (and human) rights. Reactions to treating non-human animals as persons vary widely. Some people think it is ridiculous to even entertain the idea as they feel that persons have to be human. For others, they believe the criteria of personhood includes being rational, self-aware, autonomous, having culture, and being able to communicate. Chimpanzees and dolphins, for example, display these traits and by arguing that they be given the status of persons, they will in turn be granted basic rights (e.g. chimpanzees would no longer be kept for research and could be moved to a sanctuary).

Poaching
Similar to hunting, but the animals are killed without permission or illegally.

Selective breeding
Human beings have been modifying the genes of biological organisms for centuries through selective breeding: choosing individual plants and animals with particular traits, like fast growth rates or good seed production, and breeding them with others to produce the most desirable combination of characteristics. However, unlike genetic modification, this can happen only within closely-related species.

Sentient being
Sentience is the ability to experience feelings and sensations, such as pain, distress or comfort. The Animal Welfare (Sentience) Bill includes vertebrates, but also allows invertebrates to be added through specific requirements. Recently, octopus, lobsters and crabs were recognised by the UK Government as sentient beings.

Vivisection
The act or practice of cutting into or performing surgery on living animals for the purpose of scientific research.

Index

A
activism 3, 5, 26
Animal Welfare Acts (UK) 2, 8, 15–16

B
behaviour, zoo animals 31
breeding, selective 34–37

C
cages 2, 3, 15–16
cephalopods 10, 11
cosmetics 12, 15, 23–24
cruelty to pets 40, 41

D
dogs 7, 12, 13, 34–37, 38, 40

E
elephants 29, 30, 31, 33
ethics 6–7, 18–19, 26
European Union (EU) 14
exports, live animal 16, 38–39

F
farm animals 1–3, 12–13, 14, 15–16, 38–39
Farthing, Pen 4
fashion 32
feathers 32
Five Freedoms 2–3
food, cost of 14
fur trade 32

G
Geronimo (alpaca) 4

H
health problems, dogs 34–37
hens 2–3, 14, 15
Humane League, The 1–3
hunting 33, 38

I
imports 16, 33

K
Kept Animals Bill 38–39

L
laws
  South Korea 12–13
  United Kingdom 2, 5, 15–16, 23, 38–39
  around the world 8–9, 18–19

M
medical research 23–24, 25–26, 27–28

P
pain 11, 19
pets 7, 13, 38–39, 40, 41
procedures, research 17, 20–22
products made from animals 6
public opinion 23–24

R
religions 5
rights, definitions 1, 2
RSPCA 40

S
sentience 5, 8–9, 10–11
skin trade 32
slaughter, laws 16
South Korea 12–13

T
testing, animal
  alternatives 13, 25–26, 27–28
  animals used 12, 17, 18–19, 20–21
  effectiveness 19, 26
  ethics 6–7, 18–19, 26
  procedures 17, 20–22
  public opinion 23–24
  regulation 15, 18–19, 27–28

U
United States, The 8–9, 18–19

W
welfare, definitions 1–3

Z
zoos 29–31